Preparing
Your Child
for
Dating

Books by Bob Barnes

Great Sexpectations (with Rosemary Barnes)
Preparing Your Child for Dating
Raising Confident Kids
Ready for Responsibility
Rock-Solid Marriage (with Rosemary Barnes)
We Need to Talk (with Rosemary Barnes)
Who's in Charge Here?
Winning the Heart of Your Stepchild

Preparing *Your* Child *for* Dating

Dr. Bob Barnes

ZondervanPublishingHouse
Grand Rapids, Michigan

A Division of HarperCollins*Publishers*

Preparing Your Child for Dating
Copyright © 1998 by Robert Barnes

Requests for information should be addressed to:

📘 ZondervanPublishingHouse
Grand Rapids, Michigan 49530

Library of Congress Cataloging-in-Publication Data

Barnes, Robert G., 1947-.
   Preparing your child for dating / Bob Barnes.
      p.   cm.
      ISBN: 0-310-20136-5 (softcover)
   1. Dating (Social customs)—United States. 2. Interpersonal relations in
children—United States. 3. Etiquette for children and teenagers—United States.
4. Children and sex—United States. I. Title.
HQ801.B27   1998
306.73—dc21   98-14679
                                              CIP

All Scripture quotations, unless otherwise indicated, are taken from the *Holy
Bible: New International Version*®. NIV®. Copyright © 1973, 1978, 1984 by
International Bible Society. Used by permission of Zondervan Publishing
House. All rights reserved.

Interior design by Sue Vandenberg Koppenol

Printed in the United States of America

98 99 00 01 02 03 04 /❖ DC/ 10 9 8 7 6 5 4 3 2 1

To my daughter, Torrey
As you go off to college this year, I am reminded
of what a wonderful and responsible job you have done
with your dating experience. You have made us
very proud and taught me much!

Contents

Part 1

A Generation
with No Guidelines

Chapter 1

"Can I" vs. "May I"

In April 1996, little Jessica Dubroff got an answer to both questions. Jessica had dreamed of flying an airplane across the United States. She was driven by a strong desire and an exuberance for flying. She wanted to set a record—to be the youngest person to fly an airplane across the United States.

Finally the day arrived when Jessica would begin her transcontinental flight in a small four-passenger Cessna, from Half Moon Bay, California to Falmouth, Massachusetts.

Her question "May I?" had been answered. She was given permission to try. Yes, she could.

But the answer to the more important question, "Can I?" turned out to be very different. A nation seemed excited to watch the progress of this four-foot-two-inch seven-year-old as she began an adventure normally reserved for trained adults. Those following her progress on television and in the newspapers did not know that Jessica was not ready to perform the tasks required. She didn't have the ability or the experience to cope with the dangers she would face.

Because Jessica was given permission to do something that she did not yet have the ability to do, she paid a high price. Jessica's plane crashed in Cheyenne, Wyoming, just one day after she had begun her cross-country flight, killing Jessica, her father, and her flight instructor.

Jessica is just one example of a child rushed into an adult activity. The child of today often seems caught in a culture that places adult activities in front of them. Children are able to get their hands on guns before they've been taught to control their childish tempers. Young teens are given the option of abortion before they've been taught the sanctity of life. Children of all ages are placed in front of television programs that were previously not even available for adults.

And children are being thrust into the adult arena of dating without first being taught the rules or shown the areas that are out of bounds. They lack the necessary training. They lack the necessary supervised practice. And, like Jessica, these children are being given permission to do something they do not yet have the ability to do safely. The results often are disastrous.

Dating is a relatively new phenomenon in our culture. Over a period of a little more than a few decades, the purpose, age range, and ground rules have gone out the window. Even more disastrous is the fact that the "dating referees," the parents, have allowed themselves to become powerless. Parents now stand on the sidelines watching, with no whistle to blow. One parent said, "What are the rules for dating, anyway?" It's hard to blow the whistle for a rule violation when you don't know any of the rules.

This abandonment of ground rules so often seen today crept up on parent and child alike. Historically, dating was not considered something done simply for entertainment, a minor social event. Instead dating, if there was any, was always a precursor to marriage. Dating was part of the selection process for marriage. It was never totally unsupervised or unstructured. Children were not left to decide when they should begin dating and what they should do during their dates. In the past, dating was under the control of the parents. There was a plan.

Few areas of family dynamics have undergone as major a transition as has the dating process. In fact, in most cases it's no longer a process. It's no longer a supervised activity for social growth. For the most part, parents have been pushed out of the dating process altogether. They're left in the dark, without any plan to help guide their child, to prepare their child for dating. All too often parents are left to do nothing more than answer the child's inevitable question: "May I?" And all too often, neither the child nor the parents have thought through the answer to the more important question: "Can I?"

This lack of a dating plan for our children almost guarantees tragedy. When children aren't helped in the process of picking their dating partners, they don't learn the skills needed for eventually selecting the partner they will marry. A direct result is our high divorce rate.

Whose job is it to teach our children how to date? Who is responsible to answer questions about dating, questions such as, When can I start to date? Where can I go on a date? What can I do on a date? What can't I do? Can I go out with him? Or her? What should I wear? And the question that probably won't come up: What is the purpose of dating?

When parents don't take the leadership in this area, making sure their children have the answers to all these questions, children are left to decide for themselves. And all too often, just like Jessica Dubroff, these children don't have enough information to make a wise decision. They get hurt.

When it comes to dating, every child will most certainly ask the question, "May I?" It's the parents' responsibility to provide the training so that both the parents and the child can answer the child's more significant, but unspoken, question: "Can I?"

Left to themselves, where do children get their answers about dating? Most influential in today's child's life are television, music, peers, and even their own biology.

Today's parents must step back into the dating process and prepare their children to succeed at dating. Dating is not a social "sport." Parents need to teach their children that dating has a purpose, certain goals. They need to be able to answer the question "Can I?" rather than simply giving permission by saying, "You may."

Chapter 2

Develop a Plan
Before You Develop a Problem

Jennifer was sixteen years old and yearning to please. Her parents were well aware of her "pleaser" trait and had made good use of it as a tool for motivating their daughter. In fact, parents and daughter had worked out an unspoken arrangement: When Jennifer worked hard and did her best to please them, she was rewarded. After her sixteenth birthday, Jennifer had a 4.0 grade point average on her winter term report card. She had pleased her parents so, as they always did, they rewarded her with what she wanted—a brand-new Ford Mustang convertible. This arrangement had worked well in the past and now it allowed Jennifer's parents to move on to other things they needed to do. At the time they were very busy with their other child. Younger Jeremy didn't have an ounce of "pleaser" in his body and was a constant challenge to his parents.

Left on her own, Jennifer began dating Jack, a nice boy from her school. It was her first experience with dating. Her parents weren't concerned; they knew their daughter would do what was right. She always did. They didn't even spend much time talking to Jennifer about dating because they were certain their daughter would continue along the path of working hard to please them. Unfortunately, what they had ignored was the fact that she would also work hard to please her new boyfriend. Jennifer had been taught to please the people she loved, and she thought she loved Jack. He said that he loved her. In order to please Jack, Jennifer found herself having to choose whom she was going to please. While on a date, should she please her parents and stay out of the backseat of Jack's car? Or should she please Jack, hopping in the backseat and making him happy? She knew in her heart that something was wrong with this thought process, but she was caught in a difficult conflict. She had been conditioned to please the significant people around her. She had been rewarded every time she did please them. This time, in the tug-of-war between Jack and what her parents might say, the winner would be the one who offered the most in return for her behavior.

Jennifer found herself in a situation that could be called "pleaser dating." Taught to please her parents—and rewarded for it—this system of manipulation worked well while she was a little girl, when it involved only Jennifer and her parents. As she grew older, more people became involved.

One weekend Jennifer got a ticket for speeding. The incident got blown way out of proportion, and Jennifer and her parents had a tremendous argument. Things were said; feelings were hurt. Jennifer's close relationship with her parents was damaged, and she suddenly felt at odds with the two people who had been closest to her.

For comfort, she turned to Jack. And, still being a pleaser, she unfortunately responded to Jack by pleasing him in the backseat of his car.

Pleaser dating, as a process for managing the dating scene, is very dangerous. Parent and child can very quickly end up holding each other hostage. An "If you don't . . . , I will . . ." challenge can very quickly be said. Many parents, having made that threat, wonder later how they got to that situation. Jennifer's parents wondered how their "pleaser" daughter could turn into a pregnant sixteen-year-old.

Replacement Dating

Lauri grew up in a very religious home. Her parents were pillars of the church and Lauri was at church every time there was a program to attend. An extremely affectionate girl, Lauri had spent many evenings when she was younger sitting cozily with her father while he read to her.

As Lauri grew older, her relationship with her father changed. He got busy with work and church and they rarely spent the same kind of time together. Her father also began to feel awkward having such an affectionate relationship with a teenage daughter. His equally affectionate wife explained to him that having an affectionate relationship with his daughter was natural. She even suggested that he take Lauri out on "dates," but this dad just felt funny about it. He was more comfortable buying his daughter little gifts.

Lauri didn't realize it, but she desperately missed the affection she had learned to look forward to from Daddy. As she started going out with boys, she did what seemed natural—she transferred the physical displays of affection from her father to the boy she was dating. She was very clingy, sitting on the boy's lap and touching him constantly. That was all Lauri wanted to do. It met her need for affection and replaced the affection she was missing from her father.

The physical affection—the touching—that Lauri was giving to her boyfriend might have been all she was interested in, but it made him interested in much more. It was the switch that turned on the process for even greater intimacy for her very normal, very hormonal boyfriend.

Lauri found herself in a constant battle on dates, with first one boyfriend, then another. Her boyfriends labeled her "a tease." Lauri was using a boyfriend to replace her desire for the healthy physical affection that she no longer had with her father.

As time went on Lauri learned something else about what she thought was affection. Affection to her was touch.

The tighter or more revealing her clothes, the more touching she received. To get the touches she wanted, she began walking out the front door of her home wearing one set of clothes, then changing into another, more provocative, set later. Lauri was making trades in order to replace the affection she wasn't getting at home. With her provocative clothes and her strong desire for affection, Lauri found one other thing—she found herself in trouble.

Athletic Dating

John was a typical seventeen-year-old male. Having spent much of his childhood being mentored by afternoon sports programs, he was very physical in his approach to life. The sports programs had taught him how to compete and drive to win. Nothing wrong with that. But that was only part of the mentoring he needed.

A few years prior to John's fifteenth birthday, this young man began a very traumatic journey. His father admitted to a two-year extramarital affair and left the family. John was devastated. He was further devastated by his parents' divorce. His mom, who also was devastated by the divorce, was portrayed during the divorce process as the villain even though, by all rights, she was the "victim" of the affair. Watching the divorce and how warlike it was, John's attitude toward women in general took a dramatic turn. He no longer saw them as equals. Instead he was learning that woman were to be dominated and conquered.

The television programs and movies that he escaped into during that time tended to validate that thought. The Rambo-like characters conquered any women they wanted, then left them when they were through with them. The music this fifteen-year-old gravitated toward added to this warped perspective of women. Angry rappers talking about sex and rape seemed to describe John's pain and desires.

When John began dating, the pain from the loss of his dad manifested itself in a desire to use girls rather than get to know them. All he knew about dating was only the physical. Dating became an athletic contest. Play the game. Score the touchdown. Then go on to defeat another "team" next weekend. John pictured dating as an "athletic sport," done simply for fun, at the expense of any girls foolish enough to be taken in by his winsome "half-time" show. A relationship seemed too painful, too emotional for John. That was for losers. Winning the dating game without opening up to the possibility of pain—that seemed to be the best and safest way to play the game and vent his anger. Wasn't that what his dad had done?

John was desperately in need of a nurturing relationship, but he refused to consider such a possibility. And even if he had, he would have been afraid to risk it. After all, he had seen what had happened to his parents. John was heading down the road toward a very destructive marital relationship.

Clueless Dating

Emily was growing up in a very protective home. Her parents had a well-thought-out plan for everything they wanted Emily to learn. Right from kindergarten, Emily was home schooled. Then in ninth grade they enrolled Emily in a Christian school. Her parents also decided that she wouldn't date. Instead, she would go through a courtship process when it came time for her to marry. In other words, Emily wasn't going to really date at all. Instead, the plan was to have a would-be suitor over to the house when Emily was approaching an age of marriage. Her parents thought that dating in high school was a waste of time and could only lead to trouble.

To keep Emily out of "trouble," her parents had her sign up for every possible activity. She played a sport every season at her new school. She was active in student government and very active in her youth group at church.

Because Emily knew her parents' philosophy on dating, she tried to be very careful about how she interacted with boys.

Obviously some of these activities put Emily in ongoing situations where she was with boys her age. In fact, she learned to "activity date." One year, as Emily immersed herself in the homecoming project, she got closer and closer to Brad. A very exciting and fun relationship was developing that made her feel good. She wasn't sure exactly what was happening and couldn't tell her parents about it. She knew they would be upset.

As other projects became available at school, Emily and Brad signed up to participate. Together. Brad even changed youth groups, leaving the one he was in at his church for Emily's. As the weeks passed, the two began spending more and more time together in activities with less supervision. Emily had questions about boys, but she couldn't ask her parents because she knew they'd just put her back in home school. The topic was taboo in her home.

As you might imagine, this story has an unhappy ending. But it didn't have to end that way. Emily's parents had imposed a very unrealistic policy of "no dating." They were unaware that their daughter did begin a form of dating, working on the homecoming project with Brad. Emily and Brad were "dating," but it was all going on behind the parents' backs. They had no way to supervise their daughter's dating or even discuss it with her. They couldn't acknowledge that it was going on because they didn't know about it. Emily, torn between her feelings for Brad and the ban on dating imposed by her parents, was living a lie. She suffered with a constant feeling of guilt, yet had no one but Brad to go to for counsel about her dating. Eventually Emily did have to talk with her parents when her dating progressed to the point where she had something significant to feel guilty about.

What Do These Stories Have in Common?

Though motives and emotions might be different, the common thread through all these stories is that each young person faced the dating process without one very significant element: their parents. Each child was merely thrown to the dating wolves, forced to learn how to date without being able to talk to anyone. Well, that's not exactly true. They did get some information. John got information from television and rap groups. Lauri got her information from her needs. Emily got information from Brad, the person she was dating. One young person whose story wasn't told learned everything he knew about dating from peers who were more than willing and even happy to talk about what really goes on during a date.

Parental involvement is the one element most often missing from the dating process today. No other significant area of a child's life is so unsupervised. Parents get involved in their children's science projects, homecoming float preparation, college selection, and many other worthy areas. But most parents treat dating as if it's a necessary evil that every child does eventually and over which they, as parents, have little control or input. They just hope, without actually giving their children any information, that their children will be "smart and protect themselves." Or they try to keep their children from dating altogether.

Is Dating Really That Important?

"What makes this dating thing so significant?" a parent asked after a seminar on parenting in which I had emphasized the need for parents to develop a plan for their children's dating. The first response to that question could be to encourage parents to look at the end result of dating—their child will marry a person whom they dated. If parents think it's so important to spend time helping their children make decisions about the temporary things of life, such as school courses, sports, and college, doesn't it make just as much sense—or even more—to be involved in helping their child choose the right mate? That decision is one of the most important decisions a person will ever make. It affects every other decision in adult life.

Dating should not be something a child is just thrown into. It should be a gradual process of learning, supervision, and practice.

We moved into a new house when our children were very young. It wasn't actually a *new* house, but it was new to us. As far as I was concerned the house was perfect for our family with the exception of one thing: the pool. Even though we live in south Florida, I was not at all interested in having a swimming pool, especially with a six- and nine-year-old. But like it or not, I had to accept the fact that the pool was there and had to be dealt with. Dating is a lot like that family pool.

There were basically three approaches I could have taken to our pool situation. I could have told the kids they weren't allowed to go into the pool until they were older, and thus put a verbal fence around it. That seemed to be the safest answer except for one thing: Most of our friends here in south Florida have pools and pool parties. I would have had to restrict my children from ever going to their friends' houses.

A second response could have been to say to our children, "There's the pool. I know you've never been swimming before, but I'm sure you'll figure it out. I have to go to work. Let me know how it turns out. I'll talk to you about swimming later on, when I have time. In the meantime, just jump in." Without question, that would have been a very irresponsible approach to the pool dilemma I was facing.

The third approach, and the one I used, was to develop a plan to teach my children about the pool and how to swim safely in it. There are great times and opportunities to be had with a pool, but there also are significant hazards. As a parent, it was my responsibility to set up the best plan possible to take advantage of the training opportunities.

Dating is a lot like that swimming pool. It offers parents an opportunity to teach their children about dating and how to do it safely and wisely. Dating is a natural part of cross-gender interaction—the boy-meets-girl, girl-meets-boy process. As a parent I could forbid it or ignore it, but it won't go away. It'll be there out in the open or hidden from view. Our children will be going to social gatherings and they need help in understanding the relationship they will have with the opposite sex. They need to learn all that while they're still living at home, when parents are still available on a day-to-day, face-to-face basis. Putting off instruction on dating leaves children unprepared when they go out the door to college or to full-time work. At that point they will face dating, but a parent will no longer be there to guide them or to supervise.

"That's okay!" one father said to me. "At least I will know that I got my children out the door unscathed. How my children do when they are off to college is their business. I will know that I did my best and then turned them loose."

That's not true. That father didn't do his best. That's like saying, "I'm not going to let my child drive a car while he lives at home with me. When he goes out the door to college, he'll just have to figure out that driving thing on his own." That's irresponsible parenting. Parents need to know just what areas of life their children will face when they leave home, and parents must take on the responsibility of establishing a plan to prepare each child. A concerned parent who wants to "train a child in the way he should go" (Prov. 22:6) will be diligent in training that child in the process of dating. If we don't train our children, we are setting them up to fail.

Summary

1. Left to their own devices, with no guidance from parents, teens begin dating with very immature

ideas about the opposite sex. The world around us can warp the way a teen thinks about dating.

2. When it comes to dating, teens need the guidance of their parents to combat other influences in their lives, such as television, music, and friends, that can have such a negative impact. Parents need to take the lead.

3. Parents who deny a child an opportunity to date leave that child with a tremendous handicap.

4. Parents must accept the responsibility to develop a dating plan for their children before a dating problem develops.

Questions to Ask Yourself

1. Do my children know that I have a dating plan in mind for them?

2. Who's really in charge of the dating process in our home: parent or child?

3. Do I have an answer to my child's question: when can I start dating?

4. When was the last time I sat down and talked with my child about dating?

Chapter 3

Who's in Charge Here?

Remember the dilemma I had with the swimming pool? The pool that came with the house we purchased in Florida? And my concern for our two young children who had never before lived in a house with a pool?

I got lots of advice from friends about that pool. Many even had young children about the same ages as our children. It seemed that the "challenge" of a pool brought out a variety of ways of dealing with a pool.

My overprotective dad, when he saw the house just before we bought it, went so far as to say, "You could fill the pool in with dirt and sod it over, you know. Many people do that so they can have a larger lawn for the kids to play in. In fact, in the long run it might be cheaper to fill it in than to maintain it." This grandfather just couldn't deal with the fear of placing his grandchildren so close to deep water. So before he came up with the idea of dumping the pool full of dirt, he gave me as many reasons as he could think of why we should avoid the pool problem altogether.

But taking his advice to fill in the pool to remove the danger was actually avoiding the problem because that solution would work only for our backyard. That wouldn't keep our children safe when they went to someone else's house if there was a pool. Nor would it keep them safe around the many canals so common in South Florida or at the ocean or the Gulf of Mexico. Deep water just can't be avoided in South Florida.

The opposite approach was to ignore the pool's existence, denying the danger. But that wouldn't remove the problem. Instead it would leave us vulnerable to a great tragedy.

Not a Problem, But an Opportunity

The first step in the pool dilemma is the same step that needs to be taken by parents where dating is concerned. Just as I couldn't deny that swimming pools existed and posed a risk for our children, parents can't ignore the fact that their children will have opportunities to date. Kids interact—boys with girls, in one form or another—starting in elementary school and continuing on through high school. Children will face the challenges and dangers of swimming when they are away from home. We need to teach them to swim and to take safety precautions. They'll also face decisions about dating when they are away from home, at sports activities, at school events, and at parties. They need the same kind of training for dating.

Dating provides parents the same kind of opportunity—to teach their children about dating.

If I hadn't had the pool, I wouldn't have spent as much time thinking about the dangers of the ever-present water here in South Florida. The pool that appeared to present a problem actually opened my eyes to an opportunity: "I need to teach my children how to swim!"

Teaching our children how to date is just as important. And it's not a job for the youth pastor at church or a counselor in school. It's part of our parental responsibility. But parents handle this responsibility in very different ways. In our culture the responsibility of teaching about dating is handled in one of three ways that I've labeled: Child-Directed Dating, Courting, and Parent-Directed Dating.

Child-Directed Dating

Many parents have no idea how to teach their children about dating. And some believe there's nothing they can do about it anyway. Drawing from their own dating experiences, these parents recall how they were on their own.

One father, after sitting through a parenting seminar about dating, said, "This all sounds right to me. But I just wouldn't know where to begin."

When his friend said, "You heard the speaker say how to begin. You start with . . ."

To which this father of a twelve-year-old son replied, "I guess I don't mean that I don't know how. I now have some information on how. I guess what I mean is that I don't know if I could just tell my son that I will be supervising his dating."

This man was not a reluctant leader in other areas of life. He was a partner in a large law firm, a leader. Yet strong as he was in his business life, this dad felt inept in this area of parenting. He acted as if he didn't know if he had the right to jump in and supervise his son's dating life. He didn't realize that the issue wasn't a matter of his rights. The issue was the more urgent issue of parental responsibility.

I've sometimes wondered just how such an intelligent man could become so hesitant when it comes to teaching his son about dating. And I've come up with the following scenario (obviously just a figment of my imagination) that explains this parental dilemma.

I reasoned that there must be an annual meeting that takes place every August, before school starts. It's a meeting of all middle school students. No parents allowed. In fact, parents don't know a thing about this clandestine middle school meeting. This is the meeting where the kids all take a solemn oath to control their parents. It works something like this: The kids make a pact that they all will convince their moms that their yearly science project is really not the child's responsibility, but the mom's. All a kid has to do is whimper a little, look helpless, and let it be known that the science project is due "tomorrow," and Mom accepts the assignment.

And if it works for science projects, it'll work for dating. But this time, the teens don't want any help. They don't even want Mom or Dad around. At this strategy session they plan and scheme ways to convince all parents that dating is not a topic that parents understand. Period. Phrases such as, "Don't you trust me?" "Why can't I go? Everyone else is going!" "Of course I'll drive carefully!" and "Only babies have to come in that early!" are carefully plotted and rehearsed. Note the exclamation points. Everything said by the teen on this topic requires an exclamation point. Sometimes two or three.

Sound familiar? Wonder how it got this way? For thousands of years, parents handled the dating process if there was any dating. And the dating, if it was to be done, certainly wasn't as a recreational activity. It was for the more important purpose of matrimony. Parents would get together, creating certain events and dinner parties where their young people would be able to mingle, to learn the social graces. These social events were not only arranged by the parents but supervised by the parents as well. Whatever the teens did, they did in public, under many watchful pairs of eyes.

That style of social interaction has become a thing of the past. Now, with parents removed from their children's activities, it's little wonder that some parents think their sole responsibility where dating is concerned is to advise their son or daughter to use "protection." When it comes to their children's dating, many parents have abdicated their role as trainer. This lack of training can lead to disastrous dating experiences, and without parents being involved, teens have no opportunity afterward to talk about the problems with someone they trust who can give them guidance for the future. This ultimately leads to a continuation of bad dating experiences and eventually to a poor choice of a partner for marriage.

There is a direct connection between this lack of training for dating and one of our culture's greatest problems—divorce. For two generations, this nation's parents have, for the most part, abdicated their parental responsibilities by not teaching their children how to date. Does that lead to a huge rise in the divorce rate? Of course. People make poor choices for marriage when they haven't been taught how to make a good choice. Just as there is a relationship between drunk driving and car accidents, there is a relationship between unsupervised dating and divorce. Both are irresponsible; both carry severe consequences.

I can't personally change the divorce rate in this culture. I can, however, work to do everything in my power as a parent to impact the divorce rate of my children. Child-Directed Dating is not an acceptable way to handle the dating process. It's parentally irresponsible.

Courting or Avoiding Dating

Two years ago I was preparing to speak at a Christian school in the northeastern part of this country. One of the topics of the conference was "dating." As the principal and I stood in a hall, waiting for parents to arrive, we began to discuss the topic. "Do you have any children of your own?" I asked the principal.

"Yes, I have two boys," he answered, "and I'll tell you how I have decided to handle dating ... we won't be doing it."

"You won't be doing what?" I asked.

"We won't be doing any dating. I've decided, after noticing the way these little girls are so aggressive and already calling our home, that it's just better that my boys don't date at all."

Thinking he was talking about little elementary school children, I said, "When will they begin dating?"

"They're in high school now, and they aren't permitted to date. I plan to keep it that way until we get them out of school."

That ended our discussion on his boys and dating.

Later that night the topic came up again. I was having dinner with the host couple. Somehow my conversation with the principal of the school came up. I mentioned that he had indicated that his boys did not date and wouldn't until they were out of school. The couple I was with looked at each other and then back at me. "Oh, his boys date," the man said. "It's just that he doesn't know about it. Some time ago I was picking our daughter up from a party. As I walked into the home to get my daughter, some of the kids were dancing, and the principal's son was dancing in such a sexually explicit manner that it was disgusting. Much to the embarrassment of my daughter, I walked across the room toward him. When he caught sight of me, he immediately straightened up. His son is dating. He just chooses not to know about it."

"Courting" means different things to different people. Generally it means that the young person is to be actively supervised when interacting with the opposite sex. The son or daughter is allowed to invite a friend over to the house. The two will "court" while the parents and the rest of the family interacts with them. The idea is to prevent the young couple from having any time alone where they might do something not approved by the parents. The stated goal is to give the young couple an opportunity to get acquainted in order to eventually develop a relationship that leads to marriage. The real goal is to avoid any problems before marriage, a pregnancy that would tend to force a couple to get married.

Some forms of courting don't allow the two young persons any time to be alone together, to practice setting boundaries and standards. What parents who rely on this type of courting fail to realize is that their child eventually will go away from home, where they will be going out on real dates. In fact, many of these children probably are involved in a form of "dating" at parties while still living at home. But the child doesn't tell the parents because the parents, who have insisted that only "courting" is proper, would never approve. The parents have no chance to answer a question or give advice.

Courting does have an important role in teaching young people certain aspects of dating. But in my opinion, training for dating shouldn't stop with just courting. Courting misses several important steps in the path toward successful dating. There needs to be time for a young person to practice dating away from the watchful eyes of family. There also needs to be a time for feedback, where the young person can voice delights and concerns to one or both parents.

Imagine a young woman who has never been out on a date who meets a young man in the college library. They spend time talking as they study, then he walks her back to her dormitory. He asks her out on a date that weekend. She agrees to go. She's thrilled. She's also unprepared.

This young woman has never had any practice in dating or even an opportunity to talk about dating with her parents. The subject just wasn't talked about. Her parents were "strict." Everyone knew that. She also wasn't one of the "popular" girls, and only one boy had ever asked her out while she was in high school, living at home. Her parents didn't let her go.

Now, for the first time, she's going out on a date with a young man. She doesn't know much about him. He seems nice. Shy. But how can she tell if he *is* nice? She thinks about talking with her roommates, but doesn't want them to know she's never been out on a date. They talk about all the boys they know, especially the ones they've gone out with. And when someone comes back from a date, the others just want to know what they did on the date. Sometimes she doesn't understand why they laugh. When she thinks about the date, which she does a lot, she's excited and scared. She's also on her own, with no training or guidance from her parents.

When I was a freshman in college, there were four freshman girls who, after only a semester on the campus, managed to get horrible reputations. They looked like nice wholesome girls but were among the most sexually active girls in the freshman class. When a guy in my dorm jokingly asked where these four girls came from, the reply was that all four of them had grown up overseas, in missionary homes.

To be sure, that's not always true of the children of missionaries. I should know; I married a missionary's daughter who had incredibly high standards! The difference was that Rosemary had been taught how to date. The other four missionary daughters had never been out on a date before they arrived on the campus, so they were experiencing their first interaction with young men without the benefit of any parental involvement.

Teaching a child to drive a car is a little like teaching them to date. As I write this book I am in the process of teaching my younger child how to drive a car. Robey has gotten his restricted license. This means he can only "court" the driver's seat for a year. He's not permitted to drive without having a parent with him. During that year we will be letting him drive in many different areas, but either Rosemary or I will always be in the passenger seat.

Once the year is up and he passes his driver's test, we will then begin to talk about what he can do with the car—alone. He probably will be allowed to do short test drives to the grocery store. If he does those in a responsible manner, he'll be permitted to drive farther from home and for longer periods of time, all unsupervised. We will be letting him know the same things we told his sister when she was learning. Driving the car is not one of his "rights" in any "Bill of Rights." Driving a car is a privilege! The better and more responsibly he drives, the more opportunities he gets. If he's irresponsible and doesn't go where he says he's going or doesn't do what he says he's going to do, his car privilege will be suspended for a while.

And he can expect that I'll be checking up on him. I'll want to see how he's doing. He's my child. I love him very much. I need to see how he's doing in the great battle with peers. I need to see how much more responsibility I can throw his way. And if necessary, I just might need to help him by relieving him of some responsibility. That's my job as a parent. To just hand a child the keys and say, "Teach yourself to drive and have a good time," would be irresponsible of me.

Parents wouldn't do that. They know better.

Then why don't they put the same kind of training into their children's dating? When it comes to dating, parents need to be the teachers. Parents need to be the ones who set the pace, who slow it down when necessary, all the while supervising the dating process. Parents need to prepare their young people to be ready to think through dating issues when they finally are out on their own. This means parents must allow their children the opportunity to practice dating while the parents can still hold the reins so there can be time for communication and growth.

Parents can't expect a child to be able to make good dating decisions when away from home if the young person hasn't been allowed to practice those decisions while living at home. Let your children practice dating while they're still under your roof. Encourage them to talk about their dates. Encourage them to ask you questions. Be available. Listen. Be sensitive to their needs. Today's young person, in order to become successful at dating, needs parents who are involved.

Parent-Directed Dating

The nice thing about teaching a child to drive a car is the fact that the beginning age is set by the state. Children can beg to start driving all they want, but the parent can always cop out by saying, "It's not my fault. The state won't let you drive until you're sixteen."

When it comes to dating, the first question to be answered is: who's in charge? For many parents, that's a difficult question. Without any edict on age or accepted guidelines, these parents are left to wonder about the rules and just what they should do. Some are still wondering about it when their child finally announces: "Jeff asked me to the prom. Can I go?"

Today's parents must start earlier than that. They must take charge of the dating training program for their children. The world that surrounds our young people is laced with bad advice on dating. It's not up to our children to set the standards for their lives without any input from us, their parents. Not yet, anyway. They will have to do that for themselves someday, but until then, they need guidance and practice. Until then, parents need to be teaching and preparing them for that moment when they're out on their own, as adults.

Don't expect to do this training without a fight. Remember that secret August meeting that takes place in every community? The pact among teens to take charge of their own dating? Teens won't take our parenting lying down. I wouldn't expect them to. It's the job of every healthy teen to push for more privileges! Teens are supposed to make demands. Parents are supposed to sort through the demands and set limits.

When parents direct their child's dating process, the teen probably won't say, "Oh, that's great, Mom and Dad.

I've actually been hoping you'd take this thing on and put some guidelines in my life. I can tell you, I really need them."

No, that won't happen, at least not while they're still in their teens. I have heard it said in a different way in a counseling room, however. An attractive thirty-one-year-old wished her parents had taught her more about dating. "At least that way I wouldn't have destroyed my life so early. I just asked and they just said, 'Okay.' I knew they were afraid of me. All the time I think I was pushing, hoping they would love me enough to jump into my life and say, 'No!' The harder I pushed the farther they backed away from parenting me. They had no idea what I was doing, and now that I look back I realize . . . neither did I."

The first step that parents must take is to decide to take the first step. Before anything else can be done, parents must see the need to be directing their child's progression into the dating process. Once that initial decision is made, the rest is a matter of sorting through the options that confront the young person today. Either the child will have to deal with these decisions alone or the child will have the privilege of a parent standing alongside, helping to sort through the pressures.

Summary

1. Parents may well have different reasons for setting up a dating plan for their children. The father may be uncomfortable with the whole idea of his daughter dating. The mother may want to make sure her children know more about dating than she did.
2. Parents need to set aside the time they'll need to train their children in dating.
3. In many homes, the children are in charge of their own dating. Their parents think there's nothing they can do.

4. Courting is a very controlled form of dating that does not give young people an opportunity for practicing dating on their own, away from the watchful eyes of the parents.

5. Some parents try to prevent their children from dating in high school, believing they are keeping their children safe. Instead, they're guaranteeing courting disaster.

6. In Parent-Directed Dating, the parents implement a training program that teaches their children about dating but puts the responsibility for proper dating squarely on the shoulders of the child.

Questions to Ask Yourself

1. What plan for teaching my child about dating have I adopted?

2. How have I implemented this training process?

3. What questions that my child might ask about dating will be the most difficult for me to answer?

4. How can I teach appropriate behaviors for dating as well as decision-making skills that will help my child choose wisely when they pick the person they will marry?

Part 2

The Plan for Dating

Chapter 4

Purpose and Preparation

"Okay! Okay! I hear you! But I don't know where to start."

That's the typical response from parents when talking about the plan of Parent-Directed Dating. "It's very nice that I'm going to be directing this thing ... but where do I begin?" one parent asks. That parent has begun the process. That parent has taken the first step, which is to realize the need—the purpose—of having a plan.

Too often today parents go to a seminar and hear about something they need to be doing with their children. They race home mindlessly and begin doing whatever the seminar speaker or magazine writer told them to do. If the seminar speaker told them their children need to be doing chores at home, then that's exactly what the parent tries to institute. Chores it is. That is, until the plan is challenged in some way.

When the child balks at doing chores, as children are prone to do, the plan will fold if the parents don't know the long-term reason for having the children do chores. When completing the chores becomes a hassle, a parent can easily decide it's not worth it. As one parent said, "To tell you the truth, the chore thing just wasn't working. I spent my whole weekend nagging the kids to get their chores done, and then when they finished it was a sloppy job. Why have the kids do chores when I can do it faster and better myself? Plus then we all like each other at the end of the day."

That parent had no idea what the long-term purpose was for giving a child chores to do. The purpose has very little to do with the actual chore and everything to do with teaching the concept of responsibility. Because the parent had lost sight of the reason for having children do chores, teaching chores didn't seem important. Teaching a child how to remember to take out the garbage twice a week is a great way to teach a child how to become personally responsible. It also teaches a child that being a family member carries with it responsibility. It helps a child get past the "I forgot" stage. It also ... well, you get the idea. There are many more reasons for having children do chores than simply getting a chore done. But just as soon as you forget those reasons, the plan—and the parents—cave in, and the chores are forgotten. A parent, tired by the hassle, decides it's just easier to "do it myself."

That parent has forgotten that we are supposed to be training conscious, not time conscious. It's the training that counts in parenting. The training a person receives as a child helps that person be personally responsible as an adult.

The teaching that must go along with actual dating is more important than the actual time our children will spend with a member of the opposite sex. It's more important than the event. Just as teaching a child to do chores is part of a bigger lesson, Parent-Directed Dating offers an opportunity for a child to learn lessons that will last a lifetime, skills that will become significant in a marriage. Parent-Directed Dating not only teaches appropriate behaviors for dating but also decision-making skills that help a child choose wisely the person they will marry.

Parent-Directed Dating is not just to protect a young person from getting in trouble while dating. It offers parents a great opportunity for training. Without it, parents find themselves in a position of always wanting to say "No!" when they should be saying, "Let's sit and talk about it."

Purpose

The obvious first step in Parent-Directed Dating is to spend time thinking through your own personal reasons for deciding to train your child in dating. For the two-parent home this necessitates a staff meeting. Married couples must set aside time to talk about the parental issues about which they need to make decisions. Otherwise these issues will become a great source of conflict in their marriage and in the operation of their homes.[1]

What is your purpose for setting up a dating plan? Typically each spouse, if they're honest, will have a different reason. A father of a daughter might be very uncomfortable with the whole idea of his daughter dating. If he tends to be as overprotective as I am, he would rather his daughter participate in her first chaperoned date when she's thirty years old! That would certainly have met all my fatherly needs for my own personal comfort zone. But it wouldn't have met my daughter's needs.

Mothers usually aren't as controlling. A mother might set up a plan to help a child do better at dating than the mother did, to have more information about dating, to know the seriousness of dating. A mother knows her daughter will have very romantic inclinations toward her dates. Her son will have some very strong biological inclinations. But there's another kind of son who is very compassionate, and his mother, always the protector, will want to prepare her son so that he will not be an easy mark in this day when the girl is often the aggressor.

A husband and wife need to work toward the common goal of setting up a dating plan that will benefit the training of the child rather than just keep the parents feeling comfortable. This usually takes some ongoing discussions. When you begin this process, keep in mind what end result you're looking for and how you can achieve it. Perhaps the best way to carry out this discussion is to set aside some time each week to read this book out loud together. Using the discussion questions at the end of each chapter will help you to decide where you, as a couple, want to begin the process and how you will want to proceed. There will be some issues about which you disagree. There might be some areas where you want to implement a different element to the plan. That's great! Reading the book out loud together will force this kind of much-needed discussion.

"Who has time to do that?" one parent asked after hearing in a seminar about reading books out loud to each other. "We barely have time to sit and talk to each other, let alone actually take the time to sit down and read to each other."

That statement takes us right to the crux of parenting and the value we place on it. How do we spend our time? What are we placing in our schedule that is important for parents to do? And what things are we doing that have been imposed on us? Are we training our children or just dropping them off for someone else to teach them? Are the things we do with our children just filling their time with activities and entertainment or are these activities also providing them with life-changing lessons and wisdom? Spending time training a child will impact the rest of that child's life.

Parents must decide what really counts. You can't do it all. Many parents are at the point where there's no free time in their schedule. If you're like me, you've probably said, "I can't do one more thing until I decide what I can drop."

In order to find the time I needed to train my children, I realized I could no longer serve on every committee I was asked to serve on. I even had to cut back on some of my personal recreational activities. I stopped playing golf. Actually, that decision was a little easier for me than it might be for other men. My golf game was irreparable ... downright dangerous. (I had to add that in case any of my former golf partners read this and thought, "He never had a golf game anyway," but you get the point.)

Parents who don't have enough time for good parenting (and I could have been one of them) need to take another look at how they spend their time. And when they're doing that, they should fast-forward about thirty years into the future and consider the results of that decision and what would be more important: playing golf or teaching the children?

Many parents today spend a good many hours each week chauffeuring their children from one activity to the next. They believe the activities not only will keep their children busy and out of trouble but the children will gain skills through these activities and, thus, self-esteem. Sounds like good reasoning. Everybody wins.

Involvement in activities is valuable. But when a family has no time to be a family, then a cutback in activities is in order. Parents who spend time teaching their children will have increased their children's wisdom and prepared them for life. This is significantly more important than activities that only develop their bodies and keep their time filled. There must be a balance. If not, there will be a catastrophe down the road of life.

Purpose and the Single Parent

Two questions immediately come to mind where the single parent is concerned. The first is: "Who can I discuss this with in a staff meeting? I'm doing this alone." The other is: "What if I do all this planning for a proper dating process and my ex-spouse throws it all out the door when my daughter is over there?" That's not only possible, it's probable.

But let's tackle the first question first. Since discussion about the dating process is important, the single parent needs to find someone to replace that missing partner, someone who is willing to talk about training children for dating and other issues that single parents face. For many, a group with like concerns can be a big help. For example, a church can organize a support group where single parents can meet every other week for an hour or so while sharing a potluck meal. The church can also provide another room and supervision for the children while the parent group works through the steps in setting up a plan for Parent-Directed Dating. Reading a book on parenting and discussing implementation of the principles can be very helpful. The group offers an opportunity for feedback as well as accountability.

In one such group, a single mom who was preparing her son for dating said the other group members kept her on track each week by asking her questions. They held her accountable. They gave her the support and help she needed.

Single parents also need an opportunity to discuss some things on a regular basis with a friend. One of those issues is parenting. A married friend of the same sex or another single parent would be perfect to fill the need. "But there's no time for a friend!" one single parent exclaimed in frustration at a support group meeting. That's when another woman in the group piped up with, "Darlene and I talk every night. After the kids are in bed, I either get in the bathtub or into bed and call her for our nightly check on each other. It's been a lifesaver."

Now for the second question regarding what to do when an ex-spouse ignores what you've set up as a proper dating process for your children. Single parents need to focus on doing whatever it is they can do while recognizing that there are some things over which they have no control. And an ex-spouse cannot be controlled. Generally it is the job of the custodial parent to communicate what is being done and what training is being carried on. It's a good idea to ask for some input from an ex-spouse and exchange as many ideas as possible about a child's dating. But if common ground can't be reached by the parents, then the custodial parent must move on to do the best he or she can. Don't try to control what you can't control. It will make you crazy. It will also cause you to give up.[2]

A single parent is responsible for only the parenting process in his or her own home, not in the home of the ex-spouse. That brings up an issue that offers the single parent a great opportunity while imposing a significant responsibility. The single parent might also be involved in dating, and the child will be very curious to watch how the parent handles it. That's why single parents who are dating must decide that rules and responsibilities in effect for the teen must be upheld by the parent as well.

"Oh, but that's different! I'm an adult," you might say. No, it's not different. Research shows that parents who smoke increase the likelihood of their children smoking. Young people whose parents say one thing, yet live another, have a greater chance of living the way they *see* the parents live rather than the way the parents are telling them to live. It's been said that children hear us with their eyes rather than with their ears.

"But doesn't that mean that if my ex-spouse behaves and handles dating life in an irresponsible manner, then all is lost?" No, it doesn't automatically mean that. What it does mean is that one parent must show a child how to live in a mature, responsible manner. Remember, try to control only what you can control. Don't try to control your ex-spouse.

Purpose and the Stepparent Home

In the stepparent family, there are extra dynamics to be dealt with. Parental struggles over the steps that need to be taken are often concerned with much more than the children. The arguments between parent and stepparent often are rooted in this question from the stepparent: "Who's more important to you, Honey? Me—your new spouse—or the child you've been giving in to for the last four years?"

When a stepparent is involved, nightly staff meetings are mandatory. The power games and guilt trips that the previously single parent has been dealing with are too great. Both parents in this new stepparent family must sit and talk on a regular basis about the way they are handling the decisions on their children's dating, the plan they are using for Parent-Directed Dating. If the discussions don't occur on a regular basis, the dating plan will become little more than a power game, more destructive than training oriented. And don't shy away from discussions about how everyone in the home is acting and being treated. These topics are sure to come up. And it's a good time to deal with just how everyone is feeling about different issues.[3]

Preparation

Now that you have the purpose of having a plan for dating clearly in mind, it's time to start discussing the actual plan for dating. "Is there a proper age of a child when parents should decide to have this discussion?" a parent asked. "This month" is the answer I give. It's not so much how old a child is as how well prepared the parents want to be. The more time you give it, the better prepared you'll be.

It's a whole lot like setting aside money for a child's college education or for a new home. The best time to start is now. The sooner you start a financial savings plan, the less dramatic the savings plan has to be. For example, if you start saving for a child's college expenses when the child is very young, then the amount of money that has to be put aside each month is much less than if you wait until the child is sixteen.

Start discussing your plan for your children's dating now, regardless of how old the children are. Schedule the time. Write it on the calendar. Then put together a list of questions that you want to address.

Recently I had an appointment with a financial planner. Before we could sit down to discuss my finances, the planner sent me a long list of questions he wanted me to think about and answer. He couldn't help me come up with a financial plan to get where I wanted to go until he knew what it was I was trying to accomplish.

Parents need to do the same kind of question-and-answer session in regards to their children's dating before they will be able to come up with a plan that works. Remember, there is no single right answer for any of these questions.

Questions for Parents

1. *What is the right age for a child to begin dating?* This is a question that every parent needs to think through and decide before their children answer the question for themselves. If you don't decide, the decision will be made when your child is asked to go out on a date and comes to you and says, "Can I go?" Usually, this happens when the child is younger than the parents would like. To avoid that problem, decide ahead of time and let your children know what age they must be before you'll approve of their dating.

2. *Do you think dating rules are different for your sons than they are for your daughters?* In this age of equality, there are many parents who are stumped over that question. "I feel as if I should let my daughter have the same freedoms that I should offer to my son, and yet why do I get such an uneasy feeling about that?" Equality has nothing to do with it. The rules are different because the facts are different. For example, daughters will be asked out by boys who are the same age or older. Our sons will go out with girls who are the same age or younger. That means that on a date a boy is usually

in an arena with kids his age or younger. A girl is often in a social setting with older, more experienced young people, a situation that is potentially more harmful.

3. *At what point do you think it's important to meet the person your child is dating?* Should you meet your child's date before the first date takes place? Or should you meet the person after your child has gone out with this person for a period of time? Should your meeting be postponed until after your child has become serious with this other person? Time was that when a son brought a girl home to meet his parents it meant he was serious about her. If he wasn't, he didn't.

4. *How will you help your child become wise in the selection of a date?* Will your child know whom to select for a date? Or will your child be at the mercy of whomever is doing the asking? When your child is asked for a date, does that mean he or she must say yes? We expect boys to be calling girls for a date. But is it okay for girls to call boys to ask for a date?

5. *What is the relationship between dating and marriage?* How much effect does your children's choice of whom they date have on their choice of a partner in marriage? What should your children be learning from dating that will help them in choosing a mate?

6. *How should the dating process begin?* In what ways can you prepare your children for dating? What activities are good preliminary social situations to help a child learn how to act on a date?

7. *What factors should you consider when setting a date curfew for your child?* Does it depend on the location? Your child's date? The type of date? Or on how late other kids are allowed to stay out?

8. *How does your child get a change in the regular cur-few in order to stay out later?* Is the change made strictly on age? On schoolwork? Past performance? How does a child get to the point where there is no curfew? Or is no curfew even an option? What con-sequences do you set for curfew violations?

9. *How can parents teach their sons and daughters appro-priate dating behavior?* What behaviors do you con-sider inappropriate? What guidelines will you give your children for deciding where to go on a date and what to wear? What general principles can they apply to new situations?

10. *When a child violates your dating plan, what are the consequences?* Are you certain that your child understands not only the plan but also what will happen if the plan is not followed?

11. *How will the post-date discussion be handled with your child?* Which parent is better able to listen and respond to your child's report on the date? When is the best time for this discussion with your child? If your child balks at telling you about a date, what should you do?

12. *How can you help prepare your child to have the proper response when faced with a difficult situation while on a date or at a party with a group of friends?* Some par-ents make a list of problems that their children could face, then use role-playing to practice some appropriate responses.

13. *What one basic principle do you believe is the most important to pass on to your children concerning their dating?*

These are just some of the questions that parents need to think about and discuss when their children are getting ready to date. As you delve into the subject, you'll come up with more questions. And, as you gather information, some of your ideas probably will change. That's okay. The questions here are meant to start you on your way, to provide help in the beginning and a roadmap of where you need to go.

As you review the material in this chapter, set aside some time to think about your answers to these questions and how they apply to your children. Begin to set up a plan for Parent-Directed Dating, guided by your answers to these and other questions.

If you don't take the time to answer these questions, your children and their peers will do it for you.

Summary

1. Begin the process of setting up a Parent-Directed Dating Plan by setting aside time to think through just what you believe is important for your child to know about dating.
2. Understand the obstacles you face in dealing with your child's dating if you are a single parent or a stepparent.
3. The purpose for having a clear dating plan for your children is much broader than just keeping a child from getting into trouble while on a date. A good dating plan can have positive rewards that carry over into the rest of a child's life.
4. Begin putting together a dating plan for your children by thinking through your answers to questions about dating, such as when to meet your child's date, setting a curfew, and establishing consequences for rule violations.

Questions to Ask Yourself

1. What is the right age for my child to begin dating?
2. Do I think dating rules are different for boys than they are for girls? Why?

3. At what point in the dating process do I want to meet my child's date?

4. How can I help a child become wise in selecting a date?

5. Just how much of a relationship is there between date selection and my child's selection of a spouse?

6. What kinds of dates are appropriate when my child begins to date?

7. What dating curfew will I set for my child?

8. On what basis will I change the time for my child's curfew?

9. What dating behaviors should I as a parent be teaching my children?

10. What consequences are appropriate when my child violates the dating plan?

11. What is the value of a post-date discussion between me and my child?

12. How will I prepare my child to handle difficult situations while on a date?

Notes

1. For more information on the marital staff meeting concept, read *We Need to Talk* by Bob and Rosemary Barnes (Grand Rapids: Zondervan, 1997).

2. For further information on single parenting, read *Single Parenting* by Bob Barnes (Wheaton, Ill.: Tyndale, 1992).

3. For help in working together as parent and stepparent, see *Winning the Heart of Your Stepchild* by Bob Barnes (Grand Rapids: Zondervan, 1997).

Chapter 5

Progression and Practice

When I hit the age of eighteen, my dad gave me a very special watch. It was a watch that had been promised to me. I had been waiting for it. As Dad gave me the watch, he talked about how to be careful with it. He told me it was valuable. Then, that was it. Suddenly I was free to decide when and where to wear it. The decision was all mine.

Dating isn't like that. Parents can't, in a few minutes, tell their children everything they need to know about dating. Dating is not like an object that can be replaced. It's an ongoing activity that takes both instruction and practice.

Remember when you were learning to drive a car? It took weeks of practice. You probably drove around in a parking lot at first and then progressed to a street with little traffic on it. After you had proven that you could drive safely there, you got to drive on some of the major streets, even downtown. An expressway, with its merging traffic, wasn't allowed until you had proven your driving skills in all the other situations.

Learning to date is a lot like learning to drive a car. You start out on simple dates, with other people around, and progress toward the next level. Once you've mastered that, you can again progress to handling more responsibility.

Now, as a parent, you have to be aware of not only where your child is going on dates but also with whom and what they're doing. If a child takes a step backward in handling the responsibility of dating, that's okay. Just go back a step and work on it until your child is ready to move on again.

Progression

Denise was fifteen years old and, like most girls her age, was begging her parents to let her date. To help her begin the process, her parents told Denise that there would be several steps to her dating progression, and she would be responsible for how fast she went from one step to the next.

"What do you mean I'm 'responsible'?" Denise said.

Her parents explained that they were in charge of deciding where she could go on a date and the rules she would be expected to follow on her dates. "You will be held responsible for how you do," they said. "If you do well and practice these steps successfully, then you will have earned more dating privileges. And we'll both be excited for you."

Denise gave her parents a quizzical look.

"Remember when we were teaching Jack how to drive a car?" Denise's father said. "We spent weekend after weekend in the school parking lot. He wanted to drive us to church, but we kept saying that he wasn't ready. Before he could drive the family to church on Sunday morning, there were some things he needed to be able to do in the parking lot on Saturday morning. Finally he was able to do those things and progressed to the next step of driving. How fast he progressed was up to him. Each time he learned a new skill, we gave him more responsibility behind the wheel.

"But do you remember what happened when he got that speeding ticket? For a while, he lost the privilege to drive."

Denise's parents had used the same sort of plan for their son's dating. And now it was Denise's turn. If she acted responsibly while dating, she would be given more responsibility and more privileges. If not ...

By placing the responsibility for earning more privileges squarely on the shoulders of your child, you prevent many arguments about the rules of dating. The child who doesn't come in on time after a date knows better than to ask to be allowed to stay out later than the curfew. Or, if they do ask, the parent has a good answer. "Why are you asking me? Ask yourself that question."

Parents also need to be aware of what's going on at the parties their children are attending. And they can't always depend on their children to tell them. When parents find out that a child did not act responsibly, they need to make it clear to the child just what was wrong and what the child should have done about it.

One mother, after finding out about the drinking going on at a party her daughter was at, told her daughter that she should have called to have her parents pick her up. She should not have stayed at the party. Only as the daughter mastered the different steps of dating would she earn more privileges.

The ICE Plan for Teaching Responsibility

"That sounds nice, to set up a plan and rules for dating," a reader might be thinking at this moment, "but how does a parent implement it? A plan is one thing. Getting it across to your kid is another."

A family's plan for dating lets everyone know just who is responsible for what. Without a plan, I guarantee there will be a lot of arguing and a lot of yelling and screaming. Without a plan, the parent becomes the enemy.

One method for teaching children responsibility is the ICE plan.[1] It places the responsibility where it belongs, on the young person's shoulders, and allows parents to be parents.

The ICE plan for successful parenting has three basic components: Instruction, Control, and Exercise. Instruction, the first step, teaches children what they are responsible for. Parents explain to a child just what they expect the child to do. Set the rules, the guidelines, but make the rules broad enough so that your child can't come back later to say, "But you never told me I couldn't ..."

Donna had asked her parents if she could go to a party at a friend's house after a basketball game. The game would be over by nine; Donna's curfew was eleven. Her parents had decided she was ready to go to a party of that type. They also called the parents of Donna's friend to find out more about the party.

When they told Donna that they had called, she was upset. "Oh, no! You didn't really call Linda's parents, did you? I can't believe you did that! I'm so embarrassed! I'm the only one who has parents who would actually call!" she had wailed.

"As a matter of fact you're not," Donna's father said. "Linda's mom said several parents had called. But that doesn't really matter. What does matter is that you are going to a party at the home of a person whose parents we don't know. That's why we called. Now, if you don't want us to make those phone calls, then you need to be prepared for us to tell you that you can't go to these parties. It's up to you."

Donna wasn't convinced that having parents calling other parents about a party was a good idea. But she did agree with what her father said next.

"We have decided to let you go, but here is the stipulation: You must stay at the party and be ready for us to pick you up at eleven. But if anything is going on at that party that you are uncomfortable with or that you know we don't approve of, you are to call us and we'll pick you up right away. If you don't call and we find out that something was going on at the party that we don't want you to be involved in, then we'll tighten the reins on parties. You won't be going to some."

This is a good start, but Donna's parents need to go further in helping her understand exactly what they're talking about. They need to tell her what kinds of things they consider unacceptable. "If people at the party are doing _____ , _____ , or _____ , please call us immediately."

Providing your child with this kind of instruction places on your child's shoulders the responsibility for monitoring the activities at the party and deciding what is not acceptable. It teaches a child how to think through a situation and consider the possible consequences. The child gets an opportunity to make a difficult decision. The child also gets to assess that decision (or failure to make a decision) against what actually happened. What the child learns by doing this is far more important than the party or what might be going on at the party. The child is learning problem-solving skills that will be used for a lifetime.

Too many parents do all the thinking for their children out of their sense of love and their sense of duty to protect their children. This kind of parenting leaves the child handicapped and not prepared for adulthood.

Children need to know how to think through a decision and stick with that decision despite pressure from peers. They also need to know what to do. Donna's parents told her to call them if she was uncomfortable about anything going on at the party. They'd pick her up. The decision then is not only whether something is appropriate or not but also what action to take. Do you walk away? Do you call the police? An ambulance? A neighbor? Or 911?

Parents who take their parental responsibilities seriously aren't just shooting from the hip. They're instructing their children not only on topics for conversation and proper etiquette for dating but on safety issues as well. Dating should be thought of as preparing our children for adulthood, for interacting with other people, for learning how to get along with others. The other part of that training is the practice, the actual dating.

If a young person chooses to challenge or violate parents' instructions on dating, then parents must be ready to impose a consequence (the "C" in the ICE plan), one that has been clearly explained to the child ahead of time. However, the fact that children know what to expect if they act irresponsibly has very little bearing on how they actually respond. Parents need to be prepared when they impose a consequence. Some of the more common lines kids use are: "You didn't tell me that," or "I forgot," or "I didn't know that," or "It's not fair," or "I would have been the only one to call his parents." Be prepared for the fact that your kid will try to wiggle out of the consequence. But also know that even though children might act surprised or call a penalty "not fair," they know in their hearts that they chose the wrong thing. They know they have no one to blame but themselves. And sometimes, that's hard for them to admit.

Think through the consequences you'll impose before you need them. Perhaps a daughter goes to an unacceptable party and doesn't call home for a ride. Your son says he's going one place, but actually goes to another. Or he tells you he's going to a movie and once inside switches theaters to see a film that is R-rated. What are appropriate consequences for such irresponsible dating behavior? No dating for a week? A month? Loss of telephone privileges? Extra household chores? Try to make the consequence fit the crime. Think it through beforehand. Just as we teach our children how to think through and even practice a response to a difficult situation, parents need to decide on consequences before anger and/or fear color our thinking.

Always remember, however, not to take your children's improper dating behavior personally. Your child did not do whatever it was to spite you, the parent. This is rarely the case. This is not something that your child has done *to* you. This is just something unacceptable that the child has done— period.

When parents do make the mistake of taking a child's improper behavior as a personal affront, then too often the consequences levied on the spot have to be revoked later. Oftentimes, punishments meted out in the heat of the moment are far more severe than the behavior warrants.

Exercise is the final and hardest element in the ICE plan. After instructing a child and establishing consequences for not following those instructions, parents need to allow the child the opportunity to exercise his or her options. The child needs to be given opportunities to practice making the right decisions, to practice being personally responsible. Every young person needs to be left alone to exercise the ability to think and decide. For if those skills are not exercised, they might never develop.

The ICE plan places responsibilities where they need to be. The children are given the responsibility for the way they handle their social behavior. The parents, who set the guidelines for that behavior, are responsible to deal with any improper behavior. When the young person has a setback, then parents and child know the consequences, whether it's spending Friday night at home or cleaning out the garage.

The ICE plan offers parents a way of teaching their children personal responsibility and discipline without making the parent the enemy. It obviously works better during the dating process if it has been used throughout the child's life in other areas as well.

If parents don't have a plan for dealing with the many issues that come up during their children's dating, there will be arguments—not just parent-child arguing, but parent-parent arguing as well. Arguing leads to inconsistency. Tempers flare and threats are made. Too often, parents become the enemy. When there's no plan to follow for dealing with unacceptable behavior, the yelling and screaming become the consequence. When there's a lot of arguing, parents tend to withdraw their love and their close relationship from the young person as a form of discipline. Withdrawing parental love from a child is too severe. That should never happen. When there is a good plan in place, that doesn't happen.

Practice

Remember Donna earlier in this chapter who wanted to go to a party at a friend's house? Instead of waiting until eleven to pick up their daughter, Donna's parents arrived at the home twenty minutes early, at 10:40. They rang the front doorbell and were invited in by one of Donna's classmates, who scurried off to tell Donna. The party was in full swing in the rec room at the back of the house, with some spillover into the kitchen. No adults were in sight. What they did see were some of the activities that they had discussed with Donna as being unacceptable. About that time, alerted to her parents' presence, Donna found them. She quickly grabbed her jacket and hurried her parents out of the house.

On the drive home, Donna didn't say a word. Just as Donna's dad was turning into their driveway, he said, "I was disappointed to see what was going on in that house tonight."

Donna immediately tried to defend the activities by saying that's just the way parties are these days. "Everybody does those things," she added in almost a whisper.

"Honey, that might be so, but we had already established that you would call us if any of those things were going on."

Donna knew what she should have done. Her parents had made that very clear. She just hadn't had the courage to call her parents in the middle of the party. What would her classmates have thought? What would they have said?

Donna learned a valuable lesson that night. Her lack of courage was a setback. Instead of proving to her parents that she could handle a difficult situation, she proved that she couldn't. But the party was not a failure. Donna learned that as difficult as peer pressure might be, caving in to it has even worse penalties.

Children need to learn that the consequences for improper behavior are not always the penalties prescribed by parents. Life carries its own set of penalties that often are even more severe.

Donna's parents were simply helping their daughter to learn to do the right thing, stand up for what she believed. This is even difficult for adults. If we don't help our children learn to do it when they're young and still at home, they may never have the personal strength to go against "what everyone is doing" when they're out on their own.

One Lesson Learned

One night about ten, Rosemary and I were dressed for bed, looking forward to enjoying some time together, without kids, in our den. Music was playing softly. A fire crackled in the fireplace. I had just sat down next to Rosemary when the doorbell rang. "Who could that be at this hour?" Rosemary said.

It was a logical question. Our daughter, Torrey, was at a high school party and not expected back until midnight. Robey, who was fifteen at the time, had already gone to bed, exhausted from an event at his high school.

When I opened the front door, I was shocked to see Torrey and several other kids standing there. I was too startled to say anything. I just stood there. I didn't even move out of the way so they could come in. They were supposed to be at school. Why weren't they?

"Dad, can we come in?" Torrey said, a quizzical look on her face.

"Oh, yes. Yes, I'm sorry. Come in. Just give me a second to get some decent clothes on." I pulled my robe a bit tighter.

With Torrey and her friends settled in the kitchen, laughing and exploring the refrigerator, I went to get dressed. When I returned, Torrey explained their visit. "We went to the party and there was a lot of drinking and other things. I said to these guys that you wouldn't mind if we came to our house and had our own party. Is that okay?"

My romantic night was finished, but my hopes for my daughter's future were tremendously enhanced. She had done the right thing and she had even brought others with her.

The kind of decision-making that Torrey displayed didn't happen overnight. It took years of practice. Does it mean that I will never have to deal with another dating mistake on her part? No, it means that I will always have that moment when she did the right thing. It also meant that we were ready to progress to the next step in her dating process.

Summary

1. Parents can't, in just a few minutes, tell their children everything they need to know about dating.
2. Dating is learned in steps. You start out on simple dates, with other people around, then progress toward the next level and more responsibility.
3. Use the ICE plan to deal with the responsibility of dating. The ICE plan will place responsibility where it belongs and help allow for a healthy parent-child relationship.
4. Don't be afraid to set the parameters for your child's dating. And don't be afraid to allow your child to practice dating.

Questions to Ask Yourself

1. How will I begin the dating process with my child? What is the first step in the dating progression?
2. What are the parameters that need to be set in this new dating experience?
3. What incidents warrant a phone call home?
4. What is the consequence for "going along with the crowd" when the crowd is going in the wrong direction?

Notes

1. See *Ready for Responsibility* by Bob Barnes (Grand Rapids: Zondervan, 1997).

Chapter 6

Creating the List for Marriage

"When do we begin this dating process?" a father asked. "Is there an age or a special moment that we start on this? Or do we just wait until our daughter comes to us and asks if she can go out on a date?"

Parents need to take the lead on teaching dating just as they do in directing the other areas of their children's lives. And sooner is better than later for starting each process.

For example, when does a parent begin directing a child toward college? When the child is ending his or her senior year of high school? Or back in elementary school when your children's study habits are being formed?

Parents need to start thinking about the significant areas of a child's life when the child is young and setting goals and planning the steps for reaching those goals. These significant steps in life need to be parent directed rather than child directed.

When it comes to dating, the answers to the inevitable questions must be thought through by the parents before the child asks. Be ready. And make sure your child is ready for dating. Start with simple steps: how to shake hands, how to introduce your date to someone, how to look a person in the eye when you meet them, how to hold the door open for someone. These are all skills that are expected of a person who is well-mannered. A child needs to know how to politely decline an offer, whether it's for food or an invitation, and how to suggest an activity. Knowing how to let a date know that an activity was not acceptable is equally important. One young woman, out on a first date with a basketball player she had been admiring from afar, went with him to an R-rated movie—one with scenes of graphic violence. She didn't say anything during the movie, afraid she'd spoil the date. But the next day, when he called her, she told him that she'd felt very uncomfortable because of the violence. "You know, I was uncomfortable, too," her date said. "It was pretty bad."

They both let the other know, politely, that violent movies were not the kind they liked to see. They took a stand and set a precedent for future dates.

Before your child asks if he or she can go out on a date, you need to be prepared with the right answer. It's kind of like saving toward retirement: sooner is always better than later.

"Well, that's it for me!" a reader might think. "My child is already dating, so there's nothing I can do about it now, right?"

No, that's wrong. Of course it's better if a child starts dating after receiving thorough instructions from parents, but it's never too late to provide parental guidance. A friend of mine had not thought through the music his teens were listening to. Then he read an article that convicted him of the fact that he needed to supply some better parental leadership in the area of music. After doing his homework and then having several staff meetings with his wife, they made a decision to take a stand on music. Was it easy? No, it wasn't. It's always easier to start with the right technique than it is to start wrong and make a change after years of doing something incorrectly. But it wasn't impossible and, in this case, the parents knew taking a stand was certainly worth the effort.

When should a parent begin dealing with the dating process? This decision is not dependent upon a child's age. The process should begin now. Parents can start with the question of when a child should be able to start dating. There are many stages involved in the experience of dating. Dating doesn't start with single-dating—boy and girl out on a date alone. Dating starts with cross-gender interacting. It starts with interacting with members of the opposite sex in activities at home, with friends in the neighborhood, in school, and in church. Children at an early age become aware that another child is not the same sex. They realize that boys are different from girls.

Cross-gender interaction is healthy and great practice for the future. During our son Robey's first five years of life, his best friend and playmate was the daughter of a close friend of ours. They had a great time together, playing and learning. Eventually they came to a point in their relationship where they started to enjoy doing different things. Robey wanted to spend more time playing sports and his little friend, though she tried sports, just wasn't as interested. Quite naturally they drifted apart for almost a decade. Though they were still friends, they no longer wanted to spend as much time together as they had in the past. He just wanted to play ball with other boys. She did not.

As time went on, Robey's little friend began showing an interest in spending time with boys long before Robey developed his interest in girls. "Is that natural?" a parent asked me. "Natural" might not be the right word. It appears to be a reality for girls to show an interest in boys before boys seem to be interested in girls. Generally, boys are much more physical than girls. In our culture boys develop interests and physical expressions through the many sports programs that are available. Sports activities are one of the easiest ways fathers can spend time with their sons. Boys also develop and enter puberty at an older age than do girls.

Unfortunately in our culture girls still don't have as many opportunities to express themselves as boys do. Much of a young girl's personal worth or self-esteem is still defined by whether she has a boyfriend or not. Add to that the fact that many girls develop relationship skills long before boys do. They're ready for dating before boys are. Boys read sports magazines. Girls read magazines that talk about dating. Girls talk to their friends on the phone, logging hours of practice in expressing feelings and emotions. Boys' phone time has to do with getting a ride to basketball or football practice, or to a game, or to find out the score of a game.

However, the desire to spend time with the opposite sex is being accelerated for both boys and girls in our culture. Perhaps the number-one accelerator is television. Children watch other young children on television sitcoms talking about boyfriend-girlfriend relationships. Sexual information heard and seen today by a young person watching TV was previously reserved for adults. Many taboos of the past are gone. This flood of sexual information creates a heightened interest in the opposite sex for both boys and girls at a much earlier age.

Since 1974 I have had the privilege of being the executive director of Sheridan House Family Ministries. Sheridan House has an eight-acre residential campus for middle-school-age boys and a four-acre residential campus for middle-school-age girls. These two campuses are seven miles apart.

Never do the boys say to the counselors on their campus, "Are we ever going to spend time with the girls from the girls' homes?" or "Could we get together with the girls again like we did for Thanksgiving?" That's just not a thought or a concern for boys at this age. These twelve- and thirteen-year-old boys are too busy and too sweaty from playing basketball to think about girls.

The girls, on the other hand, ask regularly. Getting together with boys has become a recurring thought for them. The girls have pictures of boys on the bulletin boards in their bedrooms. The boys have posters of athletes—all male.

When the boys from one campus got together with the girls from the other campus for a dinner in the Lodge, the boys actually combed their hair and put on cologne (enough to make breathing in the Lodge difficult). The boys worked at being "cool." The girls were . . . girls.

The boys never asked to do that again. That's not where their interest is at this age. The girls? They were ready to get together with the boys the next day.

Putting It Together

What have we said? First, parents must be the ones to begin setting up the plan for a child's dating. The parents must think through when a child should start dating. The dating process begins with cross-gender interaction. In most cases, it is the girl who is more focused on the cross-gender interaction than the boy. She wants to date and wants a boyfriend at an earlier age than he does. He might think he wants to date at an earlier age, but that is generally due to listening to friends, watching too many sitcoms on television, or the fact that a girl from his school is calling him and she is asking him out.

It's difficult for a parent to know where to begin. Should parents start by selecting an age when their child can begin dating? Should it be the same age for all children in a family? Or are some children more mature at that age than others? Should boys have different guidelines than girls?

There is a lot to consider. It's much more than simply picking an age and then saying okay, go for it. The dating process starts by helping a child think about the end result of dating. It's not simply a recreational activity. Dating does lead to something.

Be Her First "Date"

When Brenda was ten years old, her father took her out to dinner every month. Prior to that they had gone out for breakfast, just the two of them, but this father had decided it was time to get more serious about dating his daughter. This wise father wanted to be his daughter's first date.

Brenda's dad regularly took his daughter out on these "Dad Dates" for more than the experience and fun of the event. He wanted to teach his daughter how to expect to be treated like a lady. Some evenings they went to a nice restaurant, while other evenings it was fast food. The Dad Dates taught the daughter manners as well as some of the old-fashioned chivalry, such as waiting for the male to get the door at the restaurant and letting her date help her with her coat.

Brenda's brother had "dates" with their mother. He even learned to take off his baseball cap in a fast-food restaurant. These parents wanted to make sure their children learned the nuances of dating.

Date, Not Delivery of Lecture

These parent dates were structured so as not to be used as a golden opportunity to deliver lectures about the condition of the daughter's bedroom or to remind the son that he had left his father's tools out in the yard ... again. Like any other date, these times together were set up so that they would be pleasurable for the child.

"That was often very difficult for me," this father admitted. "There were times when our relationship was under considerable strain, and I didn't really feel like taking my daughter out on a date. Once she even asked me, 'Are we still going out on our Dad Date?' I knew then that I had to work hard at separating the conflict in the house from this special time we were developing together."

Parent dates are used as an opportunity to teach a child manners and how to handle oneself in a dating situation.

The parent dating also enriches the parent-child relationship. This parent dating opens the door for great in-depth discussions. The parent needs to be a good listener. Conflicts need to be left at home.

Developing the List

One of those in-depth discussions needs to be about a future partner for life. A daughter of about ten and a son of about thirteen can begin thinking through the process of character traits for their future spouse. That's right. This is the time for a child to begin developing his or her personal list of what they want in a spouse. The list might be very superficial at first, but remember, it's just a start.

The parent should explain the list, then ask the child to begin their own list about what kind of person they want for a spouse. When parent and child are out to dinner is a good time to begin the list. The child can begin writing down items for the list right there at the table, while eating.

"Honey," the dad might say, "what do you think are some of the things that will be important to you when you pick a husband?"

"Oh, Daddy, I don't even like anyone. Why do we have to talk about that?" is a possible reply. And it opens the door to explain to the daughter that she needs to think about what kind of husband she wants long before she "likes" any one person. Otherwise she might like someone who would not be a good husband for her. She needs to think about what's important in picking a husband.

"Do you remember when we were getting ready to buy our car?" the father asks. "Do you remember how your brother kept trying to tell us to go look at this car or that car? And I said to him that those cars were not the kind of cars we were interested in buying. Then he asked me what kind of car we were interested in buying and I showed him my list—a list of what we were looking for in a car. The list didn't have the name of a particular car on it. No, instead it was a list of the things we wanted in a car. After looking at several different cars, and comparing them to the list, we knew which car was right for us.

"Selecting the person you are going to spend your life with is so much more important than selecting the right car. That's why you need to think about what will be important to you when you finally decide on a husband."

That particular evening father and daughter had a great time talking about the characteristics she thought were important. She actually wrote these character traits down on a piece of paper. Some of the things on the list were not really that important, but the father wisely knew that this list would be revisited and revised regularly. After all, the daughter wasn't getting married in the near future. The items she jotted down were just the beginning of a list and the beginning of a process.

As father and daughter continued their monthly Dad Dates, Brenda was occasionally asked to bring along her list so that they could look at it. As important as the list was, the father knew not to put too much pressure on just what his daughter wrote on the list. He also knew that it was very important that the list be Brenda's list, not her father's list. The list for marriage had to be *her* list. If this father had stepped in and made comments such as, "That's ridiculous. You can scratch that off your list," then this whole process would be a waste of time. If the daughter, over the years of reviewing the list, was not permitted to have her own opinion, then she would begin to say whatever she knew her father wanted to hear and the list would become meaningless. Instead of thinking about the characteristics of a potential spouse, she would spend her dinners trying to figure out what Dad wanted to hear her say. The list must be the child's list.

The priorities of the items on the list will change from time to time. As my daughter, Torrey, developed her list, the characteristics she wrote down changed, depending partly on whether she was mad at me at the moment. She added some items and dropped others. Sometimes the qualifications she picked sounded somewhat like me, and I was pleased. Other times they sounded like the very opposite of me. But the most important qualification was that her future husband must be a strong Christian. Oh, she didn't write that down on her first list, but after she got older, she made it number one, and it stayed there.

This process helps children begin thinking about marriage and the kind of person they would like to marry. The earlier a young person starts the list, the more effort they will have put into it, the more they can relate what they see and hear to what they want—and don't want—for a future spouse. Over time, this list will grow to become a very significant template in the spouse-selection process.

Without a list of any kind, where does a young person start? Is personal appearance the only factor to be considered in a date or a potential spouse? That's often the case. The emphasis placed on looks by television, the movie industry, and newspapers and magazines would have a boy make his choice for a date based on how good a girl looks in a bathing suit. Her character or her reputation around school wouldn't matter as long as she looked great at the dance or the beach party. Without help working on a potential template, a boy in this culture is left with little else as the deciding factor other than physical appearance.

What about a daughter? How does she pick her dates? Should she be left with the option of going out with anyone who asks her? Is that how she is to find out which young man is the right one for her, by dating everyone who asks her out and picking one simply because they had a good time on their dates? No. Daughters need help from their parents to think through the character qualities and standards that are important in a husband. Otherwise, they're left to the wolves.

Preparing the list for marriage gives parents and child an opportunity to talk about characteristics that will be important and some that are even mandatory. The list offers an opportunity to begin some difficult discussions and the even more difficult process of deciding which person is right for marriage.

The list will and must change over time, as the young person grows up. Some of the "must be" items on the list might fall down to a place of simply being important, but not mandatory. Brenda's father said that for years, the first item on Brenda's list was the word *rich*. She thought the most important thing for a husband was that he had lots of money so she could have whatever she wanted. That worried her father for a long time. But after much discussion, Brenda changed her mind. She began to see how unimportant wealth was when compared to other characteristics. And since she was free to make her own decisions, Brenda, on her own, erased *rich* from her list. It was replaced with her only "must be"—that the man she would marry had to be a Christian, a strong Christian.

The rest of the items on her list were important, but not as important as her only "must be." On her list were things that she and her husband would have to agree on, such as number of children and whether she would be able to stay home and raise the children full time. But she also wanted a profession and didn't quite know how she could swing both. She didn't care what her husband did for a living, only that he would be good at it. Honesty, a sense of responsibility, and kindness also appeared on her list as time went by. Social habits such as smoking, drinking, and drugs were on the list preceded by the words "must not." The more Brenda thought about what was important, and discussed her ideas with her parents, the more she came to look at her list as very important in helping her make a very crucial decision, one that would affect the rest of her life.

Connecting the List to the Dating Process

One night my son, Robey, walked into the den where I was working and sat down. "I'm thinking about asking out a girl I met at school," he said, a grin beginning at the corners of his mouth. "She's great and I'd like to take her to Daniel's party. What do you think?"

"Have you already asked her to the party?" I always want to know if this is an after-the-fact conversation or not.

"No, not yet, but I'd like to call her tonight before someone else does."

"Well, you know what I'm supposed to ask you here, don't you? How does she fit into your list?"

"She pretty much fits, all but one thing. She's not a Christian."

That was the big one. Being a Christian was a mandatory part of our children's template for dating. If the person in question wasn't a Christian, that meant they weren't marriageable. If they weren't marriageable, why would our children want to risk their feelings on a date with that person? Everyone can get hurt. After all, the person you marry is a person you first went out with on a date.

Every parent has to decide for themselves what the next step will be. Some will step in and set a rule that their children are not permitted to date a person who does not fit the main characteristic of the template. They'll make the decision for the child, reasoning that this particular item on the list is too significant to be ignored.

Other parents will offer strong advice but allow the young person to make their own decision. It's then up to the young person whether to stick to the marriage list for dates or ignore it.

The key here is not whether one of these choices is right. The key here is for parents to decide what they believe is important and then to help their child decide. Read on. You'll get the idea.

"Oh, Dad, it's just a date to a party! I'm not going to marry her," was the response I got from my son. He knew I was right to bring up the issue, but he didn't really want to hear it. My advice was for Robey to pass on the date but develop a relationship with the girl. We advised Robey to invite her to youth group at church and get to know her that way instead of in a dating situation. Introduce her to the other kids at the youth group rather than just being alone with her.

This particular story has a nice ending. Robey did invite the girl to a youth group activity and she became involved in the group. Then one night, during a telephone conversation, Robey led her to Christ.

It's important not to isolate our children, cutting them off from anyone who is different. They do have a responsibility to interact with and befriend children of all backgrounds. There is a big difference between spending time with someone and dating. When it comes to dating, the list will go a long way toward helping a young person understand why a classmate at school with whom they are friends might not be the right person to date. Romance too often blurs the philosophical differences that we hold to be so vital. It's easier and more desirable to keep those differences in mind before romance develops.

But I'm Already Behind

"But my son is already dating and we haven't done that yet!" a parent might think. Remember, it's never too late. Yes, we all wish we had done all the things we needed to do when we were training our children. I too wish I had done more to prepare my children for life. But when you find areas where you've dropped the ball, you start where you're at. That's what I did. That's what a lot of parents have to do.

Wendy was sixteen years old and already dating when her parents attended a seminar on this topic. They became burdened that they had not spent any time helping their daughter get ready for dating. Wendy had just gone out with the first boy who asked her. Despite the fact that their daughter was already dating, Wendy's parents started providing the information their daughter needed. Wendy's father began to take his daughter out on "dates," and yes, it was very awkward at first. In fact, the first thing Wendy asked on that first outing with her dad was, "Am I going to get a lecture for something? Is that why you're taking me out?" This dad had to work very hard over a period of time to build up their father-daughter relationship.

After several dates they began to look at putting together the spouse list. At first Wendy thought it was stupid. "Humor me," her dad said. "I think this is really important. Don't just say things that you think I want to hear. What do you think is important?" They made the list and, over a period of time, Wendy began to see that the list was really her list. In their case the list actually came to be the focal point of their father-daughter outings, even though Wendy was already dating.

Eventually Wendy went off to college. One summer while home for summer break, she met a young man. They became very serious and before she went back to school for her senior year, this young man proposed to her. Wendy felt that she was in love but wanted to talk to her dad about some areas of hesitation. "When are we going out on a date again, Dad? I need to talk to you about Eric." She hadn't told her parents about Eric's proposal.

Wendy's dad made reservations for dinner, and the two went out. By this time, the two had established a comfortable father-daughter time when they could discuss anything.

After they ordered, Wendy told her father that Eric had proposed and wanted to get married the next summer. She waited for a response from her father. She didn't actually say the words, but her silence made it clear; she wanted to know, "What do you think, Dad?"

"This is a big decision, Wendy. Let's see what your list tells you. Remember, you worked on your list when you weren't so in love with Eric. It will be very objective."

Wendy read the first thing on the list, in the "must be" area, and Eric filled that requirement. She had decided that her husband must be a committed Christian and Eric was. "Well, he certainly fills number one," Wendy said. But looking down at the list, Wendy knew that Eric was not right for her. He did not fit any of the other items on her list. Her heart kept saying that maybe somehow they could work it out, but her list, right there in black and white, reminded her that all those characteristics that she had decided were important were not important to Eric. He just didn't fit.

It was a very difficult and emotional dinner for Wendy. It was even hard for her dad, seeing his daughter struggle with her feelings for Eric. By the end of the evening, Wendy had made up her mind and had even decided how to tell Eric. And her father didn't have to say a thing. The list said it all. Wendy's father had known that Eric was wrong for his daughter. He had seen many red flags in the boy's life while the two were dating. But he had counted on the list, made up over several years, to do the job and he had counted on his daughter to refer to her list. The list, which many parents might think their child had forgotten long ago, was the very thing that helped Wendy see that she would be making a big mistake if she married Eric.

A week later, Wendy ended her relationship with Eric. It was very difficult, but it was the right thing to do. This happened many years ago. Both Wendy and Eric are happily married to other people. Thanks to Wendy's list, Wendy was able to know what was the right thing to do not only for herself but also for Eric.

So you see, it's never too late to begin teaching your child about the dating process, to have your child think about just what they should be looking for in a spouse. Without that help, your child can easily fall for someone who looks good, sounds good, but would be a disaster in marriage.

Parents need to help their children establish the criteria—the list—for marriage. That's the first step in a successful dating process.

Summary

1. Parents must be the ones to take the lead in working through the dating process.
2. A parent should be a child's first "date."
3. These parent-child dates should be fun for the child. They are not a time for lectures, although over time the parent and child can start to discuss some important subjects.
4. Help your child begin developing a list of the character traits of a good spouse.
5. Make sure the list for marriage is the child's list, not a list that you as the parent have imposed on your child.

Questions to Ask Yourself

1. What kinds of activities can I plan for dates with my child?
2. What do I believe are important traits of a mate?
3. What is in the "must be" category for a spouse?
4. What are other characteristics of a spouse that are important but not essential?
5. How can I guide my children in making their own lists without imposing my ideas on them and turning their lists into my list?

Chapter 7

The Lesson of Responsibility

Responsibility is a rare but very valuable golden nugget in our society today. When you find someone who understands the concept of personal responsibility and lives by it, you have discovered two things: First, you have found a person who has received training in responsibility, probably from a parent. And second, you have found someone you can trust—with a task or assignment or just to do the right thing.

We all seem to know what responsibility is, but few want to be held to it. Too many know what they are personally responsible to do or not do, but when they are found to be violating that "responsibility," they're full of excuses as to why it's not their fault, why they should not be held accountable.

The strength of the cord of responsibility will only be as strong as the lessons and the consequences that a person goes through to learn a sense of responsibility. Sometimes that lesson is taught by a person who holds another person accountable. Sometimes the teacher is not a person at all, but a task that doesn't get done and has automatic consequences built in. April 15 is one of those deadlines that becomes a teacher of responsibility. Those who don't pay their income tax on time pay a penalty—an automatic consequence—for their failure to act responsibly. And a lesson is learned. Sometimes it takes a person several years to learn to act responsibly because the penalty wasn't severe enough the first time to force them to change. And some never change. They just keep on paying the penalty for filing late.

As a society, we don't do an adequate job today of teaching young people the concept of responsibility. Many of those automatic, built-in "teachers" that taught this sense of responsibility to children in the past have vanished. The child of yesteryear grew up accountable to do chores. At a young age children were getting up each morning to collect eggs from the chicken coop on the family farm or to restock the grocery shelves in the family store. As children grew older they were given more responsibility, often taking on the work of the parents, milking the cows or lighting the family wood-burning stove early each morning.

"Wait a minute," a reader might be thinking. "What in the world does this have to do with dating? This is a chapter I can skip! I'm interested in learning how to teach my child about dating, not life on the farm. Where's the connection?"

The connection is simple. Dating is a very significant responsibility. There is responsibility on the parents' part to develop a plan for dating, and there is responsibility placed on the young person to handle the dating in a proper manner. Each has a responsibility to that plan: the parents to establish the plan and put it into practice, and the child to learn and grow by following the steps of the plan. Both parent and child are responsible for some facets of the dating process. Personal responsibility is more important than any specific decision that will be made about dating. Children must understand the relationship between the family's rules for dating and just how their actions when dating, whether responsible or irresponsible, directly affect how well they progress from one step to the next in the dating plan. They must understand how their dating behavior today impacts their future dating opportunities. More significantly, the young person must understand the big responsibility they have concerning their own future. What they do now can dramatically impact, in a positive or negative way, their entire future and their marriage.

That's a difficult concept for many in a generation that hasn't been taught a sense of responsibility and the difference between a "right" and a "privilege." Too many young people today don't understand the relationship between behavior and responsibility. They've never been taught what to do and what not to do. They haven't been told just how their actions, their behavior, can and will impact their future. Responsibility is a difficult concept to grasp for a young person who hasn't been taught, who hasn't been expected to act responsibly, who hasn't been held accountable for some task.

On the farm it was understood that if the cows didn't get milked one morning because the young person didn't feel like it, someone had to do it. The cows couldn't go without being milked. Even the young person on the farm understood that milking was a chore that could not be postponed for long. The results were obvious and the milking was done. The young person had a responsibility to do the milking on time—not only to the parents but also to the cows. The young farmer understood that.

Parents today need to teach their children responsibility long before those children go out the front door on their first date. Dating is one of those areas where the parents are not there to supervise. Children are allowed to act on their own. They make every decision of what to do and not do on a date. Parents need to know that a child will act responsibly. But parents also need to spell out the consequences just in case the child does not follow the rules.

Responsibility Saves the Parent-Child Relationship

"Why do I now have an earlier curfew?" Jennifer asked her parents. "I thought my curfew was midnight! I'll be the only one who has to be home at 11:30."

Jennifer's parents changed her curfew, moving up by a half hour the time when she had to be home because she had been late coming home and hadn't called to ask permission.

But Jennifer, like any normal teenager, is asking why. Parents should expect the question. It's standard. The child sees only that the parents are taking something away, changing the rules.

The parental answer to this question indicates whether or not there has been a plan to teach responsibility in dating. For a moment, let's look at two sets of parents responding to a daughter we have named Jennifer. The first parents have no template for teaching responsibility. Everything is settled by argument—the parents impose a punishment or rule change, the child argues, then the parents give their arguments. It can drag on. Let's listen in. One parent is explaining the change.

"Jennifer, we have reached a point where we feel that you can't handle a midnight curfew. You never come in on time and we continually argue about it. Each time you came in late, we told you that we were going to lower your curfew, but you promised that things would be different, so we gave in and said okay." (Notice, the parent's voice gets louder.) "You *never* followed through on your promises to be in on time. This is it! You now have to be in at eleven!"

You can just picture Jennifer's response. This mythical Jennifer has been raised without any plan for teaching her responsibility. Repeatedly her parents threatened to cut back on her curfew, but then allowed her to talk them out of the punishment. Jennifer became very good at begging, arguing, pleading, even reasoning with her parents. She learned to get her way. She was rewarded for begging, arguing, and pleading instead of being rewarded for responsible behavior. Jennifer has not learned to be responsible about her curfew. What she did learn was how to disagree with her parents and convince them to let her do what she wanted to do, not what they believed was best for her. It's no wonder that Jennifer tried to argue her way out of the earlier curfew when her parents finally reached the point where they would not give in. It's also not surprising that Jennifer didn't really feel that she was to blame for the change in curfew. No, she saw it more as one more punishment imposed by her parents.

This Jennifer's parents have actually taught their child to argue rather than to be responsible. They've created an adversarial parent-child relationship. The child doesn't have to be responsible; she just has to learn how to argue convincingly. In this system (or lack of a system) the parents are teaching their child how to beat the system, how to think up ways of getting out of being responsible. The parents have become the enemy. The child learns how to get around rules. Jennifer is learning how to argue and go to war with the authority figures in her life. Under these conditions, the family relationship is put under tremendous strain.

The second set of parents uses a plan that places responsibility for proper behavior on their daughter's shoulders. Though the daughter might not like the results of her violation of the midnight curfew (and very likely will complain), her parents have taught her that she's responsible for her own actions, her behavior.

Picture the same scene again, but in a home that has a dating plan in place that teaches responsibility. This Jennifer is told that her curfew has been changed from midnight to eleven. "Why?" Jennifer asks her parents. "My curfew is midnight! I'll be the only one who has to be home at eleven!"

Notice that the two Jennifers have basically the same response. They don't want to have to come home earlier. That's natural.

But this Jennifer, who also came home late and didn't call her parents to ask permission ahead of time, knows that she did something wrong. She broke the rule. She's also been taught by her parents that there are consequences for improper, or irresponsible, behavior. We hear no arguments in the second home. Here's what we might hear:

"I'm surprised you're asking me this, Jennifer. You knew when you were late last Saturday night that the deal was you would drop back to eleven this weekend. You also know that if you are in the door by eleven this weekend, your curfew will be returned to midnight next weekend. That's the plan. You know it."

Jennifer undoubtedly brings up all the reasons for being late last weekend, excuses why she could not get home on time. It would be abnormal for her not to try to explain, hoping that maybe her parents will understand and let her get by with it just this once.

But this Jennifer doesn't have to argue with her parents. This Jennifer knows why her curfew is being changed: she came in late. She also knows that if she abides by the rules, she can earn back her midnight curfew by next weekend. But more important, the dating plan in this family has helped the parent-child relationship to remain intact.

Imagine the next step in the curfew rule. A child can be expected at some time to ask, "When will my curfew be raised to 12:30?" It's a logical question. Parents who don't have a plan in place will get asked that a lot more than parents who do have a plan for their child's dating. With no plan in place, unfortunately the entire decision rests on the parents' shoulders. The child asks and the parent says no. But finally, on some magical day after the parent has been badgered and "bad mooded" for weeks, the parent blurts out, "Okay! Okay! You can stay out till 12:30! But not a minute more!"

The lesson that young person learned was that begging, arguing, and badgering is the way to get what you want, in this case to get a curfew changed. That young person was not given an opportunity to earn a later curfew by being responsible, by coming in on time. That particular child has not learned that behaving in a responsible manner brings forth the privilege of being given more responsibility. That child has learned to do nothing more than complain and push buttons, to manipulate parents. These are not good habits to take with you into the adult world. They are especially destructive when taken into a marriage.

On the other hand, the other Jennifer, the one who has grown up in a home that teaches the concept of personal responsibility, will have the feeling of accomplishment to know that she has earned this extended curfew. She earned the later deadline because she was responsible about her curfew. When you earn it, you are more prone to protect it. Because she understands the system of responsibility, she will work harder to maintain it. Because she knows the rules, she can work successfully toward future curfew extensions until she reaches the ultimate privilege and responsibility—no curfew.

Does this mean the child will never argue with her parents? No, of course not. There will be times when the consequences connected with a plan of responsibility will be frustrating, especially when friends are able to do things forbidden by her parents. At times she'll feel that getting to the curfew she wants will take forever. But as her parents reward her behavior with small extensions of curfew, she'll begin to understand that the responsibility for a later curfew is on her shoulders. She'll be granted the later curfew after she's proven that she's responsible enough to handle it.

The Jennifer in the home that is teaching responsibility will also have another very important benefit that the other Jennifer will not have—a good relationship with her parents. Arguing doesn't work in her home. It doesn't accomplish anything. This Jennifer is learning to talk to her parents instead of trying to manipulate them. Yes, this Jennifer tries arguing from time to time, but since it doesn't accomplish anything, she quits. It's a waste of time. Instead, this

Jennifer has learned to get input from her parents on a question rather then trying to hide from her parents.

The Exceptions

With a good plan for dating in place, one that is being followed consistently by the parents, there will be times when a parent will want to give a child the benefit of the doubt. Each parent must judge the situation and decide whether an exception can be made—this once. The child who is used to a consistent handling of responsibility and personal accountability will be able to handle the fact that the plan itself can be violated occasionally. Giving a child the benefit of the doubt on rare occasions is fine as long as the parent is not just caving in and is prepared to stick to the plan in the future. Consistency actually builds the parent-child relationship. It discourages arguments. And it teaches the child a most valuable lesson—to be responsible.

The process of dating is a big responsibility. When handled by parent and child as a responsibility, dating gives a child practice in becoming personally accountable and responsible, one of the most significant lessons of life. It impacts every area of adult life. A child's dating experience can also enhance the parent-child relationship as the child looks to the parent for guidance, for understanding, and even for comfort. But as time goes on, that parent-child relationship grows and changes as the child matures. The child begins to understand the great responsibilities in marriage and parenting. Responsibility, they realize, is more than just getting a job done on time. They come to realize that they have certain responsibilities toward other people, in a variety of relationships, from the workplace to the home. This understanding of personal responsibility is of vital importance for everyone to learn. But too many adults forget—or ignore—the responsibilities they have toward a spouse, children, an employer, even to the community in which they live.

Parents can teach that sense of responsibility as they teach their children about dating and remain available while the children practice, by going out on dates. Children need an opportunity to transfer or extend the responsibility they learned in school while finishing their homework or completing science projects on time to the more adult concept of responsibility as it applies to relationships. Dating offers a more in-depth lesson on responsibility.

Where Does One Begin?

When it comes to teaching the important concept of responsibility, where does a parent start? Obviously the earlier the training is started, the easier it is for both parents and child. The young child who is responsible for certain chores at the age of five or six will find it easier to handle the responsibilities of dating when older. That child has already found out what happens when you "forget" to do a chore or don't do it on time. There is a consequence to be paid. It's logical.

This child also has learned that there are rewards for being responsible, perhaps a trip alone with a parent or being able to have a friend spend the night. Dating is just an extension of that whole idea of being responsible.

"Well, that's it for us," a parent might be thinking. "Our oldest child is thirteen and we've not done a very good job of placing responsibility on his shoulders. Is there anything we can do?"

Yes, there is. In fact, parents in this position should realize that this might be the last opportunity they have to teach their child to have a sense of personal responsibility. Though it undoubtedly will be more difficult to train a child who does not have a clear-cut understanding of responsibility, the parents need to realize the importance of this lesson. It will impact not only the choices the child makes when dating but also the choice of the person they marry. The lesson of responsibility will impact not only what to do on a date but what not to do as well. It impacts who they talk to about the decisions of life—peers or parents. It eventually will impact every area of their adult life.

Is It Ever Too Late?

Over the years, there has been a built-in plan for teaching responsibility to the young men in our society. At the age of eighteen if a young man didn't have a plan for his life (and sometimes even if he did), Uncle Sam had a plan for him—in the army. Uncle Sam drafted these young men and enrolled them in an eight-week course called "boot camp," or "basic training." At the end of that rather short but very focused period of time, each young man had become responsible for his behavior, whether or not he had known anything about responsibility when he got to boot camp. He was able to get up early in the morning, be in "by curfew," and complete his assignments on time.

No one wondered if it was too late to teach these young men or if the new recruits might be too old to learn. No, the army made the lesson of responsibility a top priority. And that's what parents need to do.

I'm not suggesting that parents put on fatigues and throw compassion out the window, like a drill instructor. I am saying that children need to learn the lesson of responsibility, and if they haven't learned it by the time they start dating, it's still not too late. It can be done. Parents need to establish a dating plan for their children that clearly puts the responsibility for behavior on the shoulders of the child. It's the only responsible thing for parents to do.

Proof Is in the Doing

Years ago I spent a summer living in the home of a very close friend. For the sake of anonymity, I'll call him Jack Russo. He was my age. He had a younger sister, Leslie, who was sixteen that summer and had her first boyfriend. The

Russos were letting Leslie date this boy, but they started the summer with a strict rule: Leslie had to be home at ten.

The night Leslie went out on her first date, the whole family, including Grandma and me, was in the family room watching a baseball game on television. Ten o'clock rolled around and Leslie was not home. At 10:15 the family began to talk about the fact that she was late. It got harder to hear the game as they became louder, more animated. Then 10:30 came and went. Still no Leslie. The parents and Grandma were furious and probably more than a little frightened by this time. Where could she be? By 10:45 Leslie's mother, father, and grandmother were talking nonstop, venting their frustrations in both English and Italian. I gave up on trying to hear the game.

A little before 11:00, when Leslie finally floated in the door, she was met by a blast of screaming and yelling. Jack and I quickly went upstairs to bed. The last words I could decipher were that Leslie was grounded for the rest of the month.

"I guess Leslie will be home watching the ball games with us for a while," I said to Jack.

"Why do you say that?" Jack asked me.

"Your parents just said she was grounded for the rest of June."

Jack said something I will never forget. He not only forecast what would happen the next night but also what it would be like for the rest of the summer.

"Oh, they didn't mean it," Jack said. "She'll talk them out of it before tomorrow night. Mark my words. Leslie will be on a date tomorrow night. Not only will she be out on a date, she'll come in when she wants to."

Sure enough, Leslie argued with her parents until they let her go out on a date that very next night. Jack also was right about her curfew. Leslie came in late that night and every other night that summer. And every night, when she came in from a date, a war broke out between Leslie and her parents.

Did Leslie win? No. Actually everyone lost something that summer. Leslie's parents became the enemy. By not sticking to the consequences they imposed, they turned their relationship with their daughter into a war zone, alienating themselves from their daughter. When they withdrew their love, as a punishment, the parents unknowingly elevated the value of Leslie's relationship with her boyfriend. The more problems she had with her parents, the more she turned to her boyfriend for comfort. The damage extended beyond that summer. As soon as Leslie graduated from high school, she got married. She had decided she was willing to do anything to get away from her parents and their ongoing war.

Leslie's parents didn't have a plan for teaching their daughter about dating. They had no method in place for teaching their daughter to be responsible for her actions. When she broke their rules, the parents imposed consequences but withdrew them when Leslie objected, quickly teaching their daughter that she could get her own way by arguing, by manipulating others. The lessons she learned in those years of dating did affect the rest of her life.

Summary

1. We all know what responsibility is, but few want to be held to it personally. Those who haven't been taught to be responsible have all kinds of excuses as to why something is not their fault.
2. Dating is a very significant responsibility. A young person is responsible for handling dating in a proper manner.
3. Parents who impose consequences when dating rules are broken, then don't follow through consistently, are teaching their children how to get their own way by arguing, pleading, and begging.

4. When parents don't require their children to act responsibly, the children learn how to argue and go to war with the authority figures in their lives. The parents become the enemy.
5. Parents need to teach their children that there are consequences for improper behavior and rewards for good behavior.

Questions to Ask Yourself

1. In what way am I helping my children to understand the concepts of responsibility and accountability?
2. What lesson am I teaching my children if I give in when they try to argue me out of a consequence I've imposed?
3. What do I need to change about the way I react when my child exhibits irresponsible behavior?
4. What responsibility can I place in my child's life that would be less volatile than dating but would be a good example of the concept of responsibility that I'm trying to teach?

Chapter 8

The Lesson of Purity

Anna sat at our kitchen table, sobbing. It was late at night. She was crying to the point where we couldn't understand a word she was saying. Anna had asked our daughter if she could talk to us, and we were trying to get to the bottom of her hysterics. Finally it became apparent that Anna needed to talk to Rosemary alone.

The girls had been on a church youth retreat for the weekend. "Nobody ever told me," she told Rosemary, brushing away her tears. "My parents never told me anything about staying pure!"

That weekend the main focus for each of the youth speakers was on sexual abstinence. No one had ever explained abstinence to Anna before. She was devastated. Finally, she couldn't take the pain any longer and asked Torrey if she could come to talk with us.

Anna's parents were very active in church. The pulpit was also a pulpit that didn't hide from teaching the truth about sexual purity. But her parents had never talked to Anna about it. Consequently, Anna had become sexually active at an early age. By the time she was halfway through high school she had slept with a boy. In fact it came out as she poured out her agony that she had slept with more than one boy.

After much coaxing, we encouraged Anna to set a time to talk with her parents about her pain. She decided to talk to her mother first, and the two of them decided that it would be best if her mom talked to her dad first, to pave the way. At first Anna's father was furious that she had done such a thing! Furious that she had told us! Furious that the youth department at the church had not had a retreat of this kind when his daughter was younger so she could have learned the lesson before it was too late! All his anger was pointed outward. It wasn't until he calmed down that he realized that it wasn't the church that had dropped the ball. He had dropped the ball.

Abstinence Is a Lesson for Parents to Teach

The teaching of the commitment to purity is an ongoing process. Parents who want to help their children learn to succeed at dating must also teach about sexuality. Some young people act as if sexual interaction is expected when on a date.

Ours is a very sexual culture. Many unthinking people have come to a point where they say sexual intercourse for teens is inevitable. We even used tax dollars during one period of time paying for a "safe sex" agenda in this country.

Sexuality cannot be ignored. Children need to know who they are sexually. They need to know how strong the sexual pull is. But most important, our children need to know the truth, and that truth comes best from the people who love them the most—their parents. Parents need to teach their children about their sexuality.

A Lesson for Boys and Girls

The lesson about abstinence is not just a lesson for girls. It is just as important for a boy to receive these lessons. For so many centuries we have placed the female gender as a prize the male wanted to "purchase" or marry, untainted by previous sexual activity. The culture treated women like property and placed the value on that property on whether a woman was a virgin. Men wanted to marry only a woman who was "pure," who had not had sexual intercourse. The same standard didn't apply to men.

Both genders need to be taught the significance of remaining pure until marriage. Both need to be challenged to adopt the discipline of giving their future spouse the gift of sexual purity. And that challenge begins with parents, explaining the responsibility each person has for maintaining that sexual purity through abstinence. Sexual abstinence is a responsibility that must be taken seriously, by the parent teaching the child and by the young person, who needs to make a serious commitment to purity that will last through the journey.

It Starts with Anatomy

"I know ... I know," a concerned father said during a discussion of sex education. "But I don't even know where to begin. My father never talked to me, and I have no idea how to talk to my son."

That father is like many parents, especially fathers. He didn't know how to talk to his son about sex because he didn't know how to use the right words—words you find in any book on anatomy, the correct words for describing the different parts of the body. They find it difficult to use the words *vagina* and *penis* at home, in private, let alone in front of their children. Even reading them here might make them feel uncomfortable.

There's a good reason for this difficulty. Their own parents weren't comfortable using the correct anatomical terms and made up nicknames for what were called the "privates." Hence we have a variety of little nicknames for the penis. Why is it we have a nickname for the penis and yet we don't feel it necessary to have a nickname for the elbow? We're comfortable with the word *elbow*.

Having a frank discussion about sex is one of the biggest areas of difficulty between spouses today. Men find it difficult to talk about sex because it's not a discussion they are used to. Oh, we do talk about our needs, but many men find it difficult to have a healthy ongoing discussion about the other person's needs, especially when it comes to asking questions using anatomical labels. For most men, that just wasn't done when they were growing up. Now that they are grown up, they feel as if they're supposed to know the answers.

Help the Child Become Comfortable with the Discussion

When teaching children about who they are sexually, parents need to use the correct names for the parts of the body that are used in the sexual experience. Children need to feel comfortable using those terms. Yes, when you teach a very young child to use the word *penis* rather than some cute nickname, you are bound to hear him scream it down the hall at church. He's probably proud of his knowledge. You should be too. But it's okay, to avoid embarrassment, to turn the other way and act like that child who just screamed "penis" for the whole world to hear is someone else's child. Don't let your embarrassment stop you from teaching your children to use the correct words.

The Next Step Is Biology

"But I'm sure my son knows all about sex," a father said. "How could anyone in this society today not have all the facts?" His statement is a sad commentary about our society, but it is incorrect. Counselors find that married couples, even after having been married for years, are still woefully uninformed about sex.

That's why parents need to talk to their children about the biology of sexuality. Children need to receive the correct information about their sexuality, not just the tidbits they can pick up in the locker room and on the playground. Our children must understand the serious issues involved in a decision to become sexually active. Sexuality is treated with such flippancy today that it requires education and frank discussion to help children understand how significant is their sexuality. Sex is not a toy to be played with as many of the music groups would have a young person believe.

All children will have questions about sex. Parents need to supply the answers, whether the children ask the questions or not. Parents need to teach their children about sexual biology to give them a foundation of information to build on. During the teenage years especially, a young person is bound to have many questions about their own development, questions about their own urges and desires. They will also have questions as to why the opposite sex seems to respond so differently. But most parents never hear those questions because it's very difficult for their children to ask questions about a topic they know little about. Most parents have not provided the information their children need about sex.

How do you change that? You make sure that your child is comfortable talking with you about sex. Which means you have to be comfortable talking about the subject. You must open the doors of communication about sexuality. You must encourage your child to ask you, the "teacher," any questions about their sexuality. You make yourself available to answer your child's questions, to discuss their concerns.

And finally you teach your child about how babies are conceived. A child who has been taught by parents to use the correct terms for the different parts of the body, who has been taught the biology of sex, will not only be comfortable discussing this with a parent but will feel comfortable asking questions. The real payoff is as adults in marriage. Those who had an open line of communication about sex with parents when they were children have a much better chance of having an open line of communication with a spouse and, as a result, a better sexual relationship.

Use a Book to Help You

For many parents, the best way to teach the biology of sexuality is to use a book as a resource. You don't just buy the book and leave it on a bedside table, hoping the child will read it. No, it's important for parent and child to read such a book together, out loud. There are many good books available today.

"Should the father read to the boys and then the mother read with the girls?" a mom asked. When my wife, Rosemary, and I conduct marriage conferences, people are sometimes surprised that we talk about the sexual aspects of marriage with men and women together, in the same room. Years ago that wasn't done. Men would be in one room with a man for a teacher, and women would be in another room, with a woman to teach them about sex. When the couples would get back together, they had no idea what each had heard. That approach didn't enhance a couple's communication about their sexual relationship. They needed to hear the information together. They needed to be comfortable not only hearing the information together but talking about it with each other.

Following that thought, we have always read Larry Christiansen's book *The Wonderful Way Babies Are Made* as a family. When parents do that, a child can feel free to ask either parent the questions they want to ask. As a matter of fact, in our family the discussions about sex have always been cross-gendered. My son, when he was very young, felt more comfortable to ask his older sister. When he got older, he asked his mother. He'd save his questions for a time when he could talk to one of them alone. He probably wouldn't have done that if he hadn't been sitting with them all the times the book was being read. Through the reading, he became comfortable talking to them about sex. The reading also gave him the opportunity to choose which family member he wanted to talk to.

The family reading of a book on sexuality opens the door for future discussions. Children might not ask any questions while sitting there on the couch with the rest of the family, reading the book together. But later on that night, in the dim light of their room, with only one parent sitting on the edge of the bed, they just might voice the question that's been rattling around in their head. The important thing is to give your children the information they're seeking and to do it in a way that lets the child know that you're comfortable with the topic. Children need to grow up feeling that they can talk with their parents about their sexuality just as they talk to you about other topics.

What Do You Stand For?

After using the correct anatomical terms when talking with your children, after teaching your children the biology of their sexuality, it's then time to talk with them about their commitment to sexual purity. That, too, is an ongoing discussion. When Robey was thirteen years old, Rosemary and I began talking to him about a great hero of the Bible.

This hero was a young Jewish boy named Joseph. God gave Joseph a dream at an early age. The dream was wrapped up in the formation of wheat stalks. Joseph didn't really know what the dream meant, but he did get the message that God had a plan for his life. The wheat stalk represented that plan to Joseph. Joseph made a decision to have a no-excuses lifestyle.

But Joseph didn't have an easy life. Joseph was beaten and sold into slavery by his brothers. Even though Joseph had to work as a slave for eleven years, only to be betrayed by his owner's wife, that didn't give him an excuse to cave in and say, "I quit." During those eleven years, Joseph didn't have any dates or even any prospects of a date. Joseph didn't take advantage of the first opportunity for sex that came to him. In fact, even though Potiphar's wife—his boss's wife—tried to coax him into a sexual affair, Joseph never compromised on his commitment to purity. He stayed pure and even went to prison because of that commitment.

Joseph became the role model we put in front of both of our children. We talked about Joseph and studied Joseph. As they learned about the life of Joseph, we told them how Joseph trusted God for his happiness, his future. They learned that Joseph trusted God to get him through the many difficult times in his life.

We also taught them that Joseph trusted that God would help him find his partner for life. And God did just that; God did his part. We taught them that Joseph's part was to stay pure, and he did his part.

As a matter of fact, we went so far as to have a piece of jewelry, a wheat stalk in the shape of a cross, made up for each of our children as a reminder of the commitment to purity that Joseph maintained.

The Ultimate Wedding Gift

Why is this purity so important? Because it's God's plan for each of us to give our spouse the gift we have been saving for marriage. Our children need to be helped to catch the vision that their purity is a gift they must protect so that they can present it to their spouse. God had a reason for including purity in his plan. God knew the emotional turmoil brought on in a marriage when thoughts of previous sexual partners intrude.

"Honey, I know you don't have any thoughts yet about who you're going to marry, but you can already start to give your spouse the greatest gift you have to give," a father might say to a daughter. "You can commit to give him your virginity. You can commit to stay pure until your wedding night." Parents need to give the same message to their sons.

Purity Needs Definition

Be prepared for your child to ask (or want to ask), "What is pure and what isn't? I mean what's okay to do and what's not okay?" Though somewhat difficult to define, it's very important to help a child think through this logical question to decide just what is okay.

No, I'm not foolish enough to give a list of what I think is acceptable. That's territory for every parent to walk through, to be responsible for. There's that huge gray area between holding hands and sexual intercourse.

Some time ago I was in a large church in a large city in the South. The church had spent time talking with the youth about the commitment of abstinence, but that was it. The young people were left with the idea that sexual intercourse was wrong. That was where you were to draw the line between okay and not okay. I was more than shocked to hear a high school girl state that they felt they were virgins if they abstained from intercourse but instead participated in oral sex. In fact, this high school senior said oral sex had almost become an expected activity if you dated someone for any length of time. "Isn't that really okay as long as you don't have sex?"

As parents we need to help our children draw a better line. There's a lot more to abstinence than not having intercourse. Young people need to be helped to see that sexual interaction begins slowly, like a train coming out of the station. It starts slowly, but then it very quickly builds up speed and it's very difficult to stop or even to slow down.

How is a young person to decide what's okay? Here's one method: If it starts the train going down the track, then it's on the list of behavior that is not okay. If it leads to further sexual activity, it should be part of the list. If it increases the passion to the point where it's difficult to slow down, it should be on the list. In reality, any activity that goes beyond kissing is hard to slow down.

"But that seems very unrealistic," a high school girl in the youth group said. "Isn't that very unfair to a boy? Isn't it unfair to stop at kissing?"

Is it more fair to lead him on? To start his train going only to stop it abruptly just before actual intercourse takes place? That kind of behavior is not fair. It's also very risky for both. At that stage, hormones may be stronger than logic.

A Vision

These decisions on just where to draw the line for abstinence need to be made before dating begins. The list of what's okay and what's not needs to be created long before the emotions of a relationship blur the vision of the list. Because that's what it is—a vision. Your children need to have a vision of the way they want to begin marriage. They need to have a clear understanding of how to maintain that vision before any dating relationship develops. They need to be able to see the danger signs. They need to know just what to say and do before they somehow find themselves in the wrong place. Like the backseat of a car.

If a young person is left to decide what the boundaries are while on a date, there will be trouble. If clear boundaries have not been set ahead of time, it's very difficult to try to draw the line at the last minute.

Purity Is More Difficult Now Than Ever Before

For thousands of years young people grew up and began puberty at about eleven or twelve. Nothing much different from this generation so far, right? Then in cultures past that young person was considered an adult at somewhere between thirteen or fifteen. In the Jewish culture, boys even went through a ceremony at thirteen. That was the boy's rite of passage into adulthood. Girls had a similar ceremony. In some cultures a boy became a warrior after he had gone out on his own to kill a lion. Adulthood and adult responsibilities and privileges came early.

So did marriage. Sometime during those early teenage years a young person was given in marriage. That left only two or three years for a young person to deal with his or her budding sexuality before actually getting married.

It was not as difficult to stay pure in those days as it is today. Not only did the young people not have to wait as long before they could engage in sexual activity but they also weren't bombarded with sexual suggestions as teens are today.

Today's young person enters puberty at eleven or twelve and generally doesn't marry until the early to mid twenties. That's more than ten years of wading through a society that has become very sexual and provocative. Huge outdoor billboards sell merchandise by using sexual innuendo. Prime-time television sitcoms have characters talking about sex. They're even shown in bed together. Magazine articles and advice columns answer just about any question a young person might have about sex. Daytime talk shows feature guests willing to talk about almost anything in their own sex lives. Sex sells. And it's not difficult for a young person's natural curiosity to be fanned into a burning desire. Hormones work that way.

Opening the Door to Purity

A young person will find it very difficult to make these decisions about abstinence alone, without any guidance from parents. And if parent and child have never had any talks about sex, they are both going to feel uncomfortable. They'll find it difficult to even use the words connected with sex.

There's a progression here, isn't there? It starts with anatomy, then moves on to biology, which opens the door to talk about purity. Within the framework of the dating progression there is a progression on this subtopic called sex. Contrary to the way many have been raised, discussions about sex are not one-time events. Discussions about sex are ongoing talks so that the young person becomes more and more comfortable discussing the topic with parents.

Sex Education and Dating Do Connect

"I only wanted to know about how to teach my child about dating. Is all the rest of this really that important?" a dad said during a seminar on dating.

Think about it. There are many components to a successful dating program. Certainly the sexual component is one of the most volatile. How could we send our children out into the world of dating without preparing them for one of the most difficult snares in the dating process? How could we send our children off to the workplace or to a college campus without first helping them prepare their abstinence list?

Notice that nothing has yet been said about when a child should start to date. Whether parents allow their child to date while in high school or believe in waiting until the child is ready for marriage, there are some components to successful dating that must be put in place. The child must begin to prepare his or her marriage partner list. The child also must have the advantage of an ongoing, parent-led sex-education program. The latter includes teaching the young person just where to draw the line when it comes to sexual activity—or behavior that can lead to sexual activity. Parents don't want to leave any of the important ingredients out of this very important training.

It's Never Too Late

Anna, the young woman who learned about purity at a youth group retreat, made some life-changing decisions that summer. With the help of her parents (after her father calmed down) and a renewed commitment to Christ, she made a decision to stay pure for the remainder of her dating life. Yes, this was a commitment that she maintained until she got married. No, it wasn't easy. This meant a new kind of dating and accountability. It meant a lot of emotional pain as her old boyfriend moved on. But it was a commitment that has blessed her new life and her relationship with her parents, especially her dad. More significantly it has blessed her relationship with her husband.

No, it's never too late to begin. The important step that parents need to take is to begin teaching their children about dating.

Some parents act as if they just want to get each child out the door without their child getting pregnant or getting someone else pregnant. That's not what we're called to do as parents. We're called to train our children, to teach them. Parents are given the task of raising the next generation to enter the adult world ready for whatever God has planned for them.

Few things can derail a child's growth as quickly as improper dating. How many people do we know who marred their lives because they became sexually active and ended up marrying the wrong person? Were forced to take just any job instead of the work God intended? When it comes to dating, a lack of sexual discipline can bring on catastrophe. Parents cannot afford to ignore the need to train their children to be sexually responsible. That training will have an impact on the rest of the child's life. We all need to strive to raise a child with the principles of a Joseph.

Summary

1. A vital part of preparing a child for the dating process is sex education, taught by the parents.
2. Start teaching your children about who they are sexually by teaching them the proper anatomical names for the different parts of the body.
3. Help your children become comfortable with talking about their bodies by discussing the topic with them.

4. Teach a child about the biology of the way babies are conceived.
5. Spend time helping your children understand the importance of a commitment to purity, to saving their body as a most precious gift for their spouse.
6. A dating education program that does not include training about sexuality is doomed to failure.

Questions to Ask Yourself

1. What books on sex are appropriate to read to my children?
2. When is the best time of the week to set aside twenty minutes to read the book on sexuality with my children in order to have time to discuss the topic?
3. Why is this important for me to do? (If you can't answer this question, you'll never do the assignment.)
4. What kind of symbol can I use to remind my children of their commitment to sexual purity?

Chapter 9

The Lesson of Safety

"Oh, Dad," my daughter protested, "you act like something is going to happen to me." This was Torrey's response when I started to talk with her about how to deal with difficult situations she might encounter while on a date.

I had been giving her a list of possible tragedies such as stalking, drugs on a date, even date rape. I wanted her to be aware of the dangers so she could protect herself. But she wasn't buying any of it. Oh, she had heard about the dangers but didn't think it could ever happen to her. She called me "overprotective" and would have preferred that I drop the whole subject.

But the subject was too important to ignore. "I don't think anything is going to happen to you, but I do want to help prepare you just in case you might find yourself in a difficult situation," I explained. "Remember when you got your driver's license and I made you learn all those safety precautions about the car? How to handle a flat tire at night? And why you shouldn't get out of the car at night? How you should lock your car door and wait for a police officer? Not one of those things has happened, but your mom and I want you to know what to do in case you do have car trouble. Dating is no different. We want you to be aware and to know what to do. Just in case."

All children feel invincible. The bad things that happen in this world won't happen to them; of that they're certain. (Aren't we all?) But sometimes an incident can teach a lesson. After Torrey started driving, a young girl in our town did have car trouble and had to pull over on the side of the road. Two young men stopped their car behind hers, saying they would help her, but forced her into their car and raped her instead.

We as parents can't afford to ignore the dangers of this world. It's our job to help our children to not only be aware of the dangers they face but also to think through a response. When out on a date, our children are vulnerable. They need to be aware of the unsafe situations that just might occur on a date.

Formulate a Plan Ahead of Time

"The first step in avoiding a tragedy is to learn to recognize certain signs and know what they mean," Jack said to his daughter Lucy.

"What are you talking about, Dad?"

Lucy's father had decided it was time to have a frank discussion with his daughter. She had gone out on a few dates, and he was worried. He was afraid she didn't know enough about boys or about dating.

"Let's say you go out with a boy you think you know pretty well," Jack said. "But as the night progresses you realize that his standards are not what you thought they were. And they're not the same as yours."

"Like what, Dad?" Lucy asked.

"You tell me," Jack replied. "You certainly know a lot more about what's going on out there than I do. What would be some indicators that someone has a different philosophy for living and dating than you do?"

By asking Lucy to fill in the blanks, Jack pulled her into the conversation. No longer was this a father giving his daughter a "lecture." Now father and daughter were discussing the issue together.

As Lucy got involved in this line of thinking, she began to realize that there were certain signals—hints—of what a date wanted to do. And she realized that some of these signals would make her feel downright uncomfortable. Even scared. She realized that it was possible her date might have very different ideas about what to do than she did.

Lucy had started with light issues, such as, "Well, I guess if he lit a cigarette, that would be the first sign that we were different." Lucy didn't smoke and didn't like being in a room where people were smoking.

Lucy had moved on to other issues. "If he took out some drugs and tried to get me to try it, that would be a shock. Or if he tried to get me to do something I don't want to do ... you know, Dad, like sex."

"That's the start of a great list, Lucy. What we need to do now is come up with a plan of how you should deal with those potential issues."

"But Dad, I would never go out with anyone like that," Lucy said, confident of her ability to judge people.

"I know you wouldn't knowingly go out with someone who would try to take advantage of you," her father said. "And I wouldn't knowingly let you go on a date with someone who I thought was going to try to hurt you. That's one of the reasons I want to meet your dates ahead of time. But we can both make mistakes. People are not always as they seem. People aren't always honest. I just want you to know what to do if you find that you are out with someone who doesn't meet your standards. I want you to know what to do. I want you to be safe."

Jack and his daughter talked about just what she should do if she ever felt that she wasn't in a completely safe situation. They talked about the different standards about drugs. About sex. About what to do if her date was drinking and intended to drive her home. About reckless driving, speeding, racing with other cars. Lucy realized that she needed a plan for each of these. She needed to know what to do so she wouldn't panic. She needed to know when to call her parents—or the police.

The discussion of safety issues and a plan of action is not just for daughters. It's a talk that sons need as well. Boys also find themselves in difficult and even dangerous social situations. They need to know what to do when a party includes drugs and alcohol, or is actually a cult activity, or when sex is offered, when the driver of the car is drunk or high on drugs, if someone in the group has a gun or a knife. A son needs the opportunity to talk through what he is going to do if his date is encouraging him to go along with the group when taking drugs, having drinking contests, or getting involved in sexual activities. His quest for manhood, driven by hormones, could take control. A young man's macho attitude, an "I can handle it" belief, has probably gotten a lot of young men in serious trouble and even killed.

Parents need to discuss with their children the dangers they could face and plan some options.

Practice a Response

We've all wished that we'd said or done something different after something happened. Hindsight is so clever. The perfect response to a coworker's rudeness forms magically on our lips about an hour later—when it's too late. *Why didn't I say that?* we moan. *If only I had . . .* is a lament we've all said. We even practice what we're going to say the next time if such a situation ever comes up again. Usually it doesn't. But we practice just the same.

And that's exactly what our children need to do: They need to practice what they'll say and do when confronted with a difficult situation before it happens. They need to think through the appropriate response so they can do what they know is right, whether it's leaving a party where illegal substances are available or refusing to get into a car when the driver has been drinking. And we as parents need to guide them.

Family role-playing can get everyone involved. Act out the various scenarios. Brother and sister can pretend they're on a date together and one could offer the other an illegal drug. A child might be at a loss of what to say, especially in front of parents. But role-playing is a great opportunity for a young person to actually practice the right words. Parents can ask questions, offer suggestions. Humor is good. I asked Robey to sit on the couch with his sister and offer her drugs. Robey decided to look the part of a "druggy" and first changed his hairstyle, slipped on sunglasses, and grabbed a jacket. The "drugs" were in a jacket pocket.

We all laughed at Robey's acting, but the topic was serious. As they tried to make their role-playing realistic, our children even corrected each other. Listening to our children, Rosemary and I realized that they knew a lot about "what was going on out there." And they taught us a lot about today's drug scene. At the end we all agreed that drugs are readily available, that each person must know how to say no.

Spending time practicing a potential response is time well spent. It might not lead a young person to the exact response that they use, but it will open the door to the possibilities. It gives a child a chance to think through what the proper response should be and why it's important. It gives a child ammunition for countering the arguments of peers. It also gives parents the opportunity to tell their children that they might be the only one who says no, but that it's more important to do the right thing than it is to follow the pack into trouble.

Recognize the Danger Signs

"Wrong place at the wrong time" is a phrase used far too many times. A good kid is arrested when police raid a party where some kids are using drugs and drinking. A girl is paralyzed when her date loses control of his car and hits a tree. He was drunk and she knew it before she got in the car.

A young person can see the early signs of a difficulty in the making. That young person has been warned by parents to "walk away" from trouble. But somehow neither message gets through. Our children want to be part of a group. They want to fit in. They don't want to seem different. And they certainly don't want to act "preachy." So they go along with the crowd until it's too late.

Talk with your children about the warning signs, the danger signals. Tell them what they should do. Start with simple things. They buy a ticket to a basketball game and get an extra $5 in change. Let them know that they'll be tempted to keep the extra $5, but that it doesn't belong to them. Right then, while still at the ticket window, they are to return the $5 and say, "You gave me too much money." Let them know how important their honesty is to the cashier, who won't have to make up the loss. Guide them in doing the right thing. Let them know the true value of their honesty.

Then discuss what your child should do when a date shows signs of heading in a direction where your child doesn't want to go. Talk about staying in a safe place, calling home if necessary. Help your child not only to recognize the signs of danger but also to make plans to stay safe.

Speak Up

Speaking up in defense of oneself is very easy for some young people, very difficult for others. Two children in the same family can be opposites. We could label one child as a "Pleaser," who just wants to please everyone. The other child might be a "Barbarian" who just wants his way. The Pleaser grows up trying to be a joy to parents. The Pleaser wants everyone to be happy. The Barbarian gives parents gray hair! The Barbarian is very demanding and challenges all the rules.

Contrary to what one might think, when it comes to dating difficulties, it is the Barbarian who will speak up when feeling unsafe. Pleasers, who have spent a lifetime trying to make everyone feel comfortable, will find it difficult to speak up or make a scene. The Pleaser feels an obligation to please his or her date.

When Elaine was a little girl, she never spent her money. She would save it for something big that she might want to buy for herself or her mom. She was a Pleaser. Her Barbarian older brother knew just how to talk her (guilt her, coerce her, beg her) into giving him her money. Even though that meant she wouldn't get to buy what she wanted, she gave in to him. She was a Pleaser.

Our children can practice the words to say in an unsafe dating situation, but not all will say them. Pleasers don't want to hurt anyone's feelings, so they have a hard time standing up for themselves, even when they could be in danger.

This is where a child's faith comes into play. A young person might not stand up for themselves, but will take a stand for God. Parents need to emphasize how important it is to stand up for what we believe in.

Vickie is a Pleaser. When she was ten, some classmates took her lunch by mistake and started eating it. She didn't want to embarrass them so she didn't say anything. She went without lunch that day.

Her mom now wants to be sure Vickie realizes that she might have to speak up for herself while she's out on a date. "Speaking up for your standards is more than just for you," Vickie's mom said. "It's taking a stand for what you believe. Many kids know that you claim to be a Christian. That's why you must speak up when you find yourself in an uncomfortable situation at a party or on a date. It will be a witness for what you believe. Don't hesitate to speak up. You're not standing up for yourself just to please you. You're speaking up to please God!"

If it's difficult for one of your children to speak up for themselves, help them find a reason. Give your Pleaser a reason to speak up. Help them to be pleasing to God.

Talk, Then Walk

When speaking up doesn't work, it's time to move—sometimes rather quickly, before it's too late—or to turn up the volume.

Barbara asked her date to take her home when drugs turned up at the party they were attending. She thought about calling her dad to ask him to come to get her, but decided she should have the guy who brought her to the party take her home.

Her date agreed and they left the party. But they didn't go straight to Barbara's house. Instead the young man drove about a block down the street and parked the car. He said he wanted to talk about the party. Barbara suggested that he just take her home and call her, that they could talk on the phone. She said she really needed to get home.

Ignoring her request, her date turned the engine off. Now Barbara was in the wrong place with a date who probably felt he had nothing to lose. He tried to convince Barbara (or force her) into making out. Right there in the car.

Barbara knew she was in trouble and pushed her date away, demanding to be taken home immediately. Her protest was ignored, so she started screaming at her date, yelling at him to take her home. In fact, Barbara protested so loudly lights were turned on in the neighborhood. She had gotten someone's attention. She knew she could ring the doorbell of one of the houses nearby and ask whoever answered to call her parents. They would pick her up.

In fact, to emphasize her point, she got out of the car and, through the open door, told her date, "All I want to do is go home. Either you take me home now or I'm going up to that house and ask them to call my parents." She pointed at the house.

Barbara's date, startled by her loud protest, had given up on the idea of sex. Her "no" did mean "no." And the last thing he needed was a set of angry parents, maybe even some threatening neighbors. When he said, "I'll take you home," Barbara got back in the car.

No doubt she was still at risk. A ride home with a disgruntled date is awkward at best and can be dangerous. But at least Barbara was taking some control of her situation. Getting out of the car and going for help to a strange house also would have had its risks. If possible, it's best to stay outside a house and have someone make a call for you.

In this case, Barbara made it home safely. The young man never called again. Barbara said later that she should have called her parents and asked one of them to come and get her from the party. Barbara was lucky. She learned to recognize a tragedy in the making and now knows what she would do the next time.

When talk doesn't work, it's time to walk.

Have a Backup Phone Plan

"Oh, no! The line is busy!"

Having more than one young person in the home means that the phone can be busy much of the time. Parents will want to think through that dilemma so that their dating young person always knows that he or she can make instant contact with "safety." For some families that might be a second phone line, one for the kids and one for the parents. For others the answer might be "call waiting" to alert whoever is on the phone at home that someone is calling.

These are both adequate options, but they work only when the parent is at home. If parents themselves are out, they are no longer available to receive a distress call. The option I have chosen is a beeper. I wear the beeper for only one reason: so my children can contact me at any time, no matter where they are or where I am. I want them to feel safe knowing they don't have to stay in an unsafe situation. I'll come and get them.

Look for a Friend

Big parties can be overwhelming to a young person just because of the sheer number of young people who are there. A mob mentality can also take over, making a young person feel unsafe.

It's always a good idea, when at a party, to look for a friend, someone you can hang out with. Parents should remind their children that one way to avoid problems is to increase the number in their own group to safely avoid anything the mob might try doing.

All these things sound logical and so much like common sense that we might feel they don't need to be mentioned. But they do need to be discussed. When an individual is in a situation where they feel unsafe or unsure of what to do, common sense often vanishes. Having discussed the options and a step-by-step plan ahead of time, a young person is more likely to stay calm and think of a safe response, the common sense approach.

A Final Escape

Let's imagine a worst case scenario. Your daughter has struggled with her date, making it clear she does not want to engage in sex. She has demanded that the young man take her home. Immediately. The young man agrees, but instead of taking her home, he drives in the opposite direction, finally parking on a lonely country road. There are no homes nearby. It's dark.

I paint this scene to emphasize that now this young woman is in grave danger of date rape or worse. Running down the middle of the road, screaming, might work. But what is to prevent the young man from driving after her? Forcing her back in the car? Or forcing her to submit at the side of the road?

Our children must recognize the first signs of danger. They must know what to do then, before it's too late. They need to understand that otherwise they might be in a situation where their very life is in danger. In some situations, there is no safe way out.

Is it unrealistic to imagine the situation I just described? Perhaps statistically it is not probable. But I have been in counseling long enough to know that many incidents of date rape have never been reported. A big factor in the date rape tragedy is the fact that the girl couldn't think of any way to escape. Later she might admit she saw warning signs but dismissed them, thinking date rape could never happen to her. She had never thought about what she should do.

I don't have a magic solution for you. The purpose for this very bleak scenario is to emphasize the seriousness of some situations. Parent and child need to talk about these kinds of situations as "possible dangers." Prepare for them. Recognize the dangers. That kind of honest discussion can avert a tragedy.

If Tragedy Happens

Cindy was sitting in my counseling office, discussing the problems in her marriage. She had been married three years. The main problem, she said, was of "a sexual nature." Suddenly she burst into tears and out came her story, a story she had never told anyone, a story of a rape that took place when she was seventeen.

The rape was horrible enough. Equally tragic, however, was the fact that she had been carrying this nightmare all alone for almost a decade. She had never told anyone—not her parents, not her husband—and her secret was destroying her marriage.

Children need to be assured of our parental love, no matter what happens. Tell your children: "If something horrible or very difficult were to take place in your life, do you know that we love you enough that you could come and tell us? Because if you don't know that now, I want to make sure you know that you can trust us to always love you no matter what. You could come and tell us anything. We love you very much and want to help you deal with anything that happens in life."

Our children also need to be able to give us signals, or "tragedy alerts." Some young people won't be able to talk to their parents. Oh, they'll want to talk, but they just can't start the conversation. They can't put it into words. Instead, they'll be more moody than usual or withdrawn. It's a signal. It's almost as if they are saying, "Something tragic has happened, but I can't tell you about it. Don't believe me when I say that nothing is wrong. Sit with me, ask me questions, and hear the real answers that are hidden beneath my denials. Be patient. Eventually I'll get it out."

When tragedy strikes, we as parents want to be available to help our children overcome the difficulty, no matter what it is. Above all, no matter what happened, we will want to make sure they know that they are loved.

Just a Precaution

A friend of ours, Steve Canfield, a police officer, always puts on his bulletproof vest before he goes out the door to drive to work. He doesn't expect to be shot at. But it's a possibility. And the bulletproof vest is a precaution. Steve has been trained to handle emergencies.

Parents need to train their children to handle the emergencies of dating. The children might see their parents as "overly protective," but it's really a matter of making children aware of what could happen and giving them the information they need to be able to recognize danger and to avoid it.

Summary

1. Help your child begin thinking about what he or she would do if they found themselves in a social setting where they felt unsafe.
2. Practice with your child a possible response to various unsafe social situations. Role-play each situation so your child can actually practice using the words. To make it less awkward, make it fun.
3. Discuss some of the possible dating danger signs, the things to look for before an incident takes place.
4. Teach your child to know when it's time to talk and when it's time to get up and walk out.
5. As difficult as it is to even imagine, talk with your child about a worst case situation. What should they do? How could they avoid it?
6. Make sure that your young person knows that no matter what happens they can always talk about it with you. You will always love them, no matter what happened.

Questions to Ask Yourself

1. When is the best time to have this kind of a difficult discussion with my child?
2. Where is the best location? Should it be at the kitchen table, in my child's room at bedtime, at a restaurant? How can I establish some place that would be good for a discussion of this type?
3. How can I begin such a discussion to help my child sense my concern and yet put my child at ease to talk?

4. What possible solutions or escapes can I think of so that my child feels as if there are some answers to difficult dating situations? How can I get my child to understand that sometimes, there is no magic solution and the best approach is to avoid the problem?

Chapter 10

The Word "Appropriate"

My kids used to hate the word "appropriate." When they would ask if it's okay to do something or go somewhere or wear something, we would always ask them if they thought it was "appropriate." It's always the final part of the template we have used to help them make decisions. "Can you do it?" I might respond to their request, "You *can* do it, but the real question is, is it appropriate?" It used to make their blood boil. *Appropriate* is a thinking word. It makes a person analyze who they really are and what they stand for. In the past, our society as a whole believed that there were things that just weren't done. They were deemed inappropriate. We've lost that common guidance system of the appropriate. Society no longer teaches or sets the standard of what is appropriate or inappropriate. And we no longer have our aunts and grandmothers living down the street from us, ready to help teach it. We don't have any automatic "appropriate" enforcers. Parents have to make the decision to teach this concept. And parents will often feel alone in this teaching process. It's a battle. It's a battle because we've hit a point where propriety now clashes with our society.

Picture this scene:

"I couldn't believe the dress her daughter had on last night," Nancy said at the dinner table.

"What do you mean?" her husband asked.

"Well, didn't you see the dress Donna had on? It was as tight as you could possibly get it and so short that it barely covered that seventeen-year-old's bottom. She looked like a French street walker. I couldn't believe that her mother let her out of the house like that."

"Maybe her mother didn't know," the husband responded in defense of the other mother.

"Didn't know!?!" his wife blasted. "Her mother was standing right next to her!"

Can't you picture this scene? This type of conversation, concerning one situation or another, probably has taken place in most homes. This one focused on a difference of opinion about what is appropriate to wear in public and what is not. That standard varies from family to family, sometimes from person to person inside the family.

As a culture we don't want to think anymore. We would prefer that someone tell us all the answers. Tell us what to do, then we can take it from there. But that won't work for "appropriate." Appropriate requires thinking and judgment.

As far as the discussion about the short dress was concerned, there was more here than simply the very subjective word *appropriate*. Another word was key in their conversation. They used the word *know*.

The husband suggested that perhaps the seventeen-year-old was able to get out of the house dressed the way she was because her mother didn't "know." He meant that the mother might not have known which dress the daughter was wearing. The wife said the mother did; she was standing right next to her daughter. But the husband may have been right after all. Perhaps the mother didn't *know* what is appropriate for this generation to wear. Perhaps the mother allowed her daughter to wear the dress because she didn't know it was inappropriate.

Or maybe the mother of the seventeen-year-old didn't know something else. Perhaps the mother knew or felt that the clothing was inappropriate but didn't know how to explain it to her daughter or didn't know how to tell her daughter that she couldn't go out of the house in an outfit like that. Perhaps the mother just didn't know how to handle the situation.

Knowing what's appropriate is a very personal decision, yet one parents can't leave up to their children, without any parental guidance. Most young people have two main sources of input, the entertainment industry and their peers. Well, there are other sources, such as popular teen magazines. But none of these do an adequate (or should I say appropriate) job.

It should not surprise any parent to see their teenager attempting to push the boundaries of what is appropriate. Teens are "designed" to stretch the limits. What is surprising is how many parents fail to help their teens think through what is appropriate.

The difficulty with teaching a young person what is appropriate is that standards and styles change. Situations are different. Clothing that is okay to wear to one type of event is not okay to wear elsewhere. We can't put all the "rules" in writing. Knowing what is appropriate is the result of a thought process and a standard rather than a list of do's and don'ts.

"But That's What Everyone Does"

Picture that same conversation at the dinner table. A mother and a father are discussing the way a particular friend's daughter was dressed at a party. All of a sudden their thirteen-year-old daughter says, "But what's wrong with the way she was dressed? I thought she looked great. Her dress was just like the one on TV last night. On . . ."

To a child, the dress was not "provocative," it was "in style." She had seen it on TV. Whether the dress was appropriate for a high school party was not a consideration. She had not yet learned that concept.

I will never forget being a chaperon at an after-dinner party for high school seniors. The party took place at a location that was miles from the formal dinner. I stood near the door with some other parents as the young couples began arriving at the party. One mother, who also was a chaperon, met her daughter at the door and walked with her into the bathroom to help her daughter change out of her formal dress. When the daughter reappeared, we were shocked. That mother had actually helped her daughter change into the tightest, most provocative "outfit" possible.

What statement was this mother-daughter team trying to make? Certainly not one that was appropriate.

It's a Statement

The concept of what is appropriate to wear and what is not is a very important one to teach our children. It's much bigger than a set of rules. What we wear broadcasts who we are. What people around us see on the outside is the first (and sometimes the only) way they judge what is on the inside.

Therein lies the first step in teaching the concept of appropriateness. Who are we and what do we stand for? Each parent needs to think through the answers for themselves. Appropriate by what standard? In the words of a great Jewish leader named Joshua, ". . . as for me and my house we will serve the Lord."

"Oh, great," a young teen might say, "that means we will be wearing togas to school."

No, it doesn't mean that we should dress like the people of Joshua's age. But it does mean that our template for what is appropriate and what is not will first be judged by the question, "Does this serve the Lord's purpose in my life?" As a family that has chosen to be visible Christians, we have to ask ourselves: "Would Christ be happy with me being at such and such a place or doing such and such a thing or wearing this? If he could see me now, would he be pleased?" "Would the Lord approve?"

We then should ask ourselves: "What does my participation in this activity say about who I am?" "By wearing this outfit or these clothes, what am I broadcasting about who I am?" Everything we do in life says something about who we are. If we claim to stand for one thing but dress in a way that says something else, then we are not consistent. Will this bathing suit give someone the wrong impression about me? Will it make someone think that I am broadcasting or advertising something that I'm not? If so, then either I'm a liar, a tease, or just stupid.

Teach, Don't Mandate

It is important to discuss—not mandate—the many areas that come under the heading of appropriateness. Discussions teach the decision-making process. Mandates teach nothing but perhaps sneakiness. We want our children to learn to think so they can eventually make those decisions for themselves. The key word here is "eventually."

Dress: There are different clothes that are appropriate for different places. We dress one way when it's just family at home and another when there are guests in the house. The fact that we permit a daughter to dress one way at home does not mean we endorse that way of dressing. It only means that we think it's okay at home. Our daughter had a tight pair of jeans with a hole the size of a dime in the seat. A patch had been sewn on the inside, but if you didn't look too closely you might think you were seeing her panties through the hole. Even though you couldn't see her panties, it looked like you could.

"So who cares?" you might say. "If it's not really her underwear who cares?"

We do. The fact that the patch looks like panties makes those jeans inappropriate for wearing out the door. What would Christ say? What does it say to the onlooker about what I stand for? For us the jeans fail those two questions.

What is being worn in public today has, in far too many instances, become very sexual, seductive. Of prime importance for our young people is the type of clothing that is appropriate on a date. What does a person's choice of clothing say about them on a date? What does a young person's choice of bathing suit say about what they want to show off at a pool party?

A young girl who is excited that she is finally developing a body cannot be expected to do a good job of making these decisions without input from her parents. She's finally growing up and excited about how she looks. But she's naive about what her bathing suit is saying to the boys at the pool party. Without meaning to, she might be advertising what the boys would like her to do rather than who she really is.

A major topic throughout the training process for successful dating must be deciding what clothing is appropriate, what message we are sending by what we wear. Some parents reading this section are going to be disappointed to find that there's no chart telling them exactly what is appropriate dress in the various situations. Other parents will say, "This is ridiculous. This is a new world we live in! The old standards just don't apply anymore."

To the parent who's looking for a list of what is appropriate, there is none. Instead, each person needs to ask the questions that correspond to their own philosophy of life.

To the parent who thinks it is unnecessary for them to set standards of appropriateness in dress, I suggest this question: Who will teach your young person if you fail to teach them what is appropriate? The latest rock star? The latest teen idol? The problem is that these celebrities are putting on a show to further their own careers. They don't care about your child. They're selling themselves. Teaching your child what is appropriate is your job.

Public Displays of Affection

Jack and Lee Ann had their daughter Annie invite her boyfriend Billy to attend a crafts fair with the family. Billy was from their church, and Jack and Lee Ann thought he was a great guy. They saw the crafts fair as a good opportunity for them to spend some time getting to know him better.

Annie had always been an affectionate young girl and was very comfortable with physical affection, with touching and hugging. She was also very excited to have a new boyfriend, and as they walked through the fair with her parents, she was all over Billy. Annie held Billy's hand, then had her arm around Billy, then as they looked at something going on, they were hugging. She ran her fingers through his hair. To Annie it wasn't sexual; she was just showing affection.

All this took her parents by surprise. They knew their daughter was very affectionate. At home, with the family, the affection had been normal. They just hadn't thought that it could create a problem.

"What do you think we need to do about this?" Jack asked Lee Ann.

They had watched with growing concern as the physical display progressed. Jack fumed and his wife tried to calm him down. But they never said a word to their daughter or to her boyfriend. Ever.

As Annie's and Billy's relationship progressed over the next few weeks, so did the affection. Annie had a television set in her room. With other friends, she just took them upstairs into her room, and they all sat on her bed watching TV. So it was natural for her to invite Billy to watch TV in her room. When her father objected, Annie flared back with, "Why, Daddy? Don't you trust me? Nothing's going to happen!"

To keep the peace between father and daughter, Annie's mother intervened. "Just keep the door open," she said.

Later, as the parents traced the progression of the inappropriate, they told of many more incidents where they simply didn't know what to do. They felt in their hearts that their daughter's displays of affection were inappropriate, that lying on the bed with her boyfriend was inappropriate, but they couldn't think of a good answer to their daughter's explanations, so they just gave in. Now the daughter was in charge and the inappropriate became the rule.

Billy and Annie spent many evenings watching TV in her room, sitting or lying together on her bed. They left the bedroom door open, so it was okay. One night, when Billy brought Annie home from a date, Annie's parents weren't home yet. The two let themselves in the house and went to Annie's room. A few weeks later, Annie realized she was pregnant.

Set Some Parameters

Our young people expect us to help them to know what's right by setting some parameters in their lives, guidelines to help them make decisions while out on a date. These guidelines can cover everything from displaying affection in public to where to go on a date. The following list gives some of the areas where we as parents need to apply some definitions of the word *appropriate*:

- Appropriate physical contact in public
- Appropriate physical contact on a date
- Appropriate places to be with a date
- Appropriate ways to sit in a car
- Appropriate places to be with a date in the home
- Appropriate ways to act with a date in the home

"But how does a parent get into a discussion about these topics?" a parent asked at a seminar.

I understand the problem. When we start talking with a child about what is appropriate, the child very likely will tune us out. They don't want our input. They make it clear that we don't know what things are like in today's world. We don't understand. They're offended because we don't trust them.

Some parents won't talk about what's appropriate; they just set rules. Others don't do either and seem surprised when they end up with sexually active young people.

Parents need to get beyond all the roadblocks and discuss just what is appropriate for all the areas of dating. It's mandatory.

You might write down a list of questions to discuss with your children at dinner. Read each question and talk about it, then encourage your children to give a response to your answer. Make it fun. Make sure your children don't think you're just laying down rules. Here are some examples.

- Do you think it's appropriate for a boy and girl to hold hands in public? If yes, when is it appropriate? When it is not appropriate?
- Do you think it's okay or appropriate for a boy and girl to walk in public with their arms around each other?
- Do you think it's ever appropriate for a boy and girl to kiss in public? What kind of kiss might be appropriate?
- What do you think would be inappropriate for a boy and girl to do in public? Why?
- Do you think there are places that are inappropriate for a boy and girl to spend time together?
- Where is it inappropriate to be when in the house?
- Where is it inappropriate to be when out in public?

- Where are other places that would be inappropriate to be?
- What places would be appropriate?
- What topics might be inappropriate for a boy and girl to talk about when on a date?

The list can go on. There are so many things that parents must decide or help their children to decide. How long is it appropriate to talk on the phone? Is it appropriate for a girl to call a boy? (Does the girl who keeps calling the boy understand that the boy no longer can enjoy the fun and intrigue of the chase?)

Parents should make their own list. They will learn much by listening to the responses of their children. The key is to listen and discuss and listen some more. End by making it clear to your children what you believe is appropriate. Just remember that the younger children who are sitting at the table, listening, are learning too. You're laying the groundwork that will be needed when they start dating.

Be prepared for a battle. Everything around your children tells them to respond to their passions and feelings. Think through why your stand is what it is and then bring them to the foundations for why you think something is inappropriate. First, does this serve the Lord's purpose in my life? Second, what statement does participation in this activity say about who I am?

Appropriate cannot be measured by what everyone else is doing. We have hit the point where propriety clashes with our society. Don't give up. It's the parents' job to set the standards for what is appropriate.

A True Story

"Mom, is it okay for me to tell Cindy that I love her?" fourteen-year-old Danny asked one night. Danny had been spending the whole summer with this new "friend" and it was obvious that they liked each other. A lot. Danny's mother was sitting on the edge of his bed when he asked the question. Danny told his mother that because they were going back to school, he really wanted Cindy to know that he liked her a lot ... before the other guys had a chance at her.

"Well, Danny," his mother began, "this is really a matter of what is appropriate and what is not. I personally think it would not be appropriate for you to tell Cindy that you love her. That's a very powerful word that you will want to save for a very special time. I personally decided not to tell that to anyone until I met your father in college. And that was after we had dated for two years and it became apparent that we were thinking about marriage. Some people use the word *love* as if it doesn't mean anything special. But that doesn't leave any word to use when they want to tell that special person that they are more special than anyone else. I think it would be inappropriate for you to tell that to Cindy."

As much as he wanted to tell Cindy that he loved her, Danny held off. He was learning about the word *appropriate*, which at the time seemed hard to understand. But if Danny were to read this section today, he'd laugh. He'd also be grateful for a mom who taught him what was appropriate back then. Danny has had several significant friends in the last several years. But none so special that he's felt it appropriate to use that special word—*love.*

Summary

1. We are a society that has lost the old concepts of what is appropriate and what is not.
2. Our children need help to understand the concept of what is appropriate. If parents don't teach it, our children will be strongly influenced by TV, movies, and popular music.
3. Teaching the concept of what is appropriate is an ongoing lesson that takes many open-ended discussions.

4. Deciding what is appropriate has to do with what you stand for, what you believe in, and who you are as a family.

Questions to Ask Yourself

1. What behaviors do I, as a parent, feel are appropriate and inappropriate for my children as they interact with the opposite sex?
2. What clothing do I feel is inappropriate? Under what conditions?
3. How can I initiate discussions with my child that will begin teaching the concept of appropriate?
4. What is the basic philosophy of life that guides me in deciding what is appropriate, what statement I'm making by my actions?

Part 3

The Dating Process

Chapter 11

Group "Dating"

"When does actual dating begin? I mean, when do we actually take the leap and let our children begin to date?"

The answer: Actual dating gets started before we realize it's gotten started. Before our children go out on a date or a double date, they practice interacting socially with the opposite sex in groups. A natural time for that to begin is during middle school. This is the time when they will begin asking for that interaction. There is a lot of peer pressure for younger children to talk about wanting to interact with the opposite sex, but the time to begin the "practice sessions" is middle school.

"Sometimes I wonder if I should even let my child go to those middle school parties," a parent lamented. "Part of me says that it's time to let go and yet another part of me worries about what goes on at those parties."

That parent was right on both counts. The middle school parties are great opportunities for kids to begin interacting in a social setting that's less structured. But many times the parties include objectionable activities or behaviors. Some middle schoolers report that they learned to smoke cigarettes, and much worse, at a middle school party. There is a broad degree of variance in the parties. The peer pressure of twenty middle schoolers gathered in one room can be overbearing for some children. But the opportunity for healthy, structured interaction is very valuable. This is actually the beginning of "dating."

The phrase "let go" that the parent used is not the proper approach. Some parents just throw in the towel and say, "What can you do anymore? We might as well just let them go. Everyone else does." Even knowing that a particular party could very likely involve very objectionable activities does not keep some parents from giving their permission to attend a party. They're unable to say no. They just feel helpless. They make the decision to "let go."

Other parents consider all parties off limits for their children. These parents either had some bad experiences at parties or have heard about objectionable activities and want to keep their children safe. But these parents are losing out on training opportunities. When will their children ever be able to practice interacting with the opposite sex in a social setting? The fact is, they won't, at least not with their parents' approval.

Both approaches miss a great opportunity of teaching. What's needed is balance, a chance for a young person to practice social interaction when they're out from under their parents' supervision. They're going to do that every day and every night when they're out of the home, in college or on the job, living in an apartment.

How Do You Find a Balance?

Remember, learning to date is a process. Instead of parents letting go, turning their kids loose, they need to be letting out some string while remaining attached. It's like flying a kite. As the kite does better and better in the wind, you don't just let go of the string. If you did, the kite would get tangled in trees or wires, or run out of wind and crash. Instead, you let out more and more string. The better the kite flies, the more string you let out.

It's not a decision that is made once and lasts for all times. It's not something you just do and that's it. It's a process. And opportunities for cross-gender interaction are a valuable part of that process.

First, parents need to decide that they are going to do some homework. Gather information from sources beyond the child. "Oh, I don't think I could do that," one parent said. "It would make my daughter furious if I made phone calls about the party." If a parent chooses to use their middle schooler as the only source of information, a parent could be led to believe that they are the only mom or dad who is not letting their child go to a certain party. The child needs to know that parents care enough to do their homework. There might be too much peer pressure on a child to be at a certain party, making it very difficult for the child to tell the parent all the details surrounding the party. Some children might even be relieved for the parents to do the necessary homework and say no, thus relieving the child of the burden of having to make the decision. "I can't go, my mom called their house and found out that . . ." Or "My parents won't let me go." These are both nice answers that take a lot of the peer pressure off young shoulders. A child might be internally relieved that she is not allowed to go to a particular party, but the parent should never expect to hear the child say thanks. It will be a rare child who will come and say, "You made the right decision, Mom. Thanks." In fact the child will be more likely to try to make the parents feel as if their child is the only eighth grader in the entire state who will not be at this particular party.

I remember one parent almost bursting into tears of joy when she found out that we had kept one of our children from going to a particular party. That mother was doing her homework and called us to ask what we knew about an eighth grade party. "I was feeling so bad," she said. "Julie had led me to believe that she was the only eighth grader who wasn't getting to go to that party. I knew in my heart that the party was the wrong place for her to be, but she really made me feel like I was destroying any possibility she would ever have for a social life."

That particular parent was so isolated she didn't realize there were dozens of other parents who were keeping their eighth graders from the party. And in this case those parents were very grateful, as the party ended up being raided by the police. The party was at the home of a very prominent family in town, but it was an unsupervised party.

When a child comes home with an invitation to a middle school party, do your homework by making the necessary phone calls. But remember two things: It's easy and comfortable to say "no" all the time, even if the party is not bad. It's easy to say no, but it can be great training to say yes, when you can. Collect the information before you make a decision about a party.

Process the Information Together

A major purpose of this early part of the dating process is to help teach a child how to properly interact in a social setting as well as with the other gender. It's an opportunity to begin the process while the child is still at home, under the parents' tutelage. Another purpose or opportunity here is to help teach a child discernment. Children need to learn to think and eventually make decisions for themselves.

In other words, don't dictate. After making the phone calls and deciding that your middle schooler cannot go, don't just make the announcement. Instead, after doing the background work, the parent should sit down with the child and together they should process the information. Though the parent needs to always have the final say, the child needs to be a part of the thinking and decision making. There are some areas for discussion, though parents will want to establish the nonnegotiable areas.

It's amazing how much each family will vary as far as what they feel is acceptable and what is absolutely out of the question. "After all these years of going to church together," one parent exclaimed with disgust, "I was just amazed to hear that so-and-so let her daughter go to that party. When I asked her if she knew that they were going to be ..., she said she knew and didn't really have a problem with it."

Everyone's list of things that are unacceptable is different. Our differences in opinion never become more volatile than when it pertains to decisions about our children. Some parents don't care if the parents will be home when a party is going on. Other parents draw the line there. Some parents feel that dancing today has gone over the line of fun and on into a sexual display, or "foreplay," as one parent described it. Some parents feel they need to have a relationship with the parent giving the party; others do not. The list of differences goes on and on.

Who is right and who is wrong? Are some parents going overboard? Others far too lenient? We are all responsible to make our own informed decisions concerning our children. Tragedy lurks when a parent chooses not to be informed. It is equally tragic when parents choose to be informed but don't have the courage to confront their child in order to make the decision they know in their hearts they should be making. The key is not to judge other parents or to be swayed by another parent's opinion. The key is to do the necessary homework, discuss the information with your middle schooler, and then make the decision of what is right for your child.

"Do any of your books have a list of things that a parent should decide are an absolute 'no' as far as permission to go to a party is concerned? What do you think?" one parent wanted to know.

It really doesn't matter what I think. What does matter is what each parent thinks. It's important to think through your own list, set your own guidelines, and then be able to explain them to your child. Not everything we do requires an explanation. But our children need to understand the logical reasons behind the decisions we make. Understanding the reasoning will give them the tools to help them make their own decisions when they are out on their own. Whether they make good decisions or not later on in life is their business. Giving our children the training and an understanding of decision-making skills is the parents' business.

At some point our children are going to be sitting in an apartment or dormitory room far from home. The phone is going to ring or someone is going to walk down the hall and invite them to a party. Children who have had all their decisions made for them and never had the opportunity to sit and process the information with a parent are left with two decision-making options: They can either call home and ask permission to go or just go since there is no longer anyone to stop them.

The young man who has sat at the table with his parents, discussing each party while going through middle school and high school, has a definite advantage. He might not have always been happy with the discussion or the decisions that were made, but he now has the skills to be able to ask the right questions about the party. He also has the skills to think through the information on his own, since he had been put in that position while at home. Then the rest is up to him. Does he want to use the skills of personal responsibility that he was taught? At least he has those skills available to him.

Think through your list of what is appropriate. Be available to adjust it from time to time. Then make the necessary phone calls to collect information on the current request. Together parent and child can then use the template for decision-making they have been developing to determine whether the party is appropriate or not.

Always remember that your discussion with your child is really bigger than the one party being discussed. Your discussion is building a decision-making template. The parent who takes the time to do the homework, make calls, find out what's going on, and then discuss the party with the child is giving that child an important gift for the future. That gift is an ability to make choices and decisions based on information, not blindly. That gives the child a great advantage over many other young people as they all enter the adult world.

Opportunities for Practice

Middle school parties offer an opportunity for many things to take place. Some of those opportunities can be damaging. That's why homework needs to be done. But to simply say that we will keep our children busy doing other things so they can't interact with the opposite sex is very unrealistic. It also misses an opportunity—an opportunity for practice.

Many families also have the golden opportunity of a great church youth group. A good middle school youth group provides a child a chance to practice interacting with the opposite sex in a safe environment. The best part about this particular setting is that it will be focused on activities and personal growth rather than being sexually oriented. Parents should look for an active middle school program at church for their young person. Just be aware that some of these groups have a very cliquish core group, making it difficult for a new person to break in. Help your child get to know other kids in the group by getting to know the youth leader. Consider volunteering your home for a youth group activity (get lots of sleep beforehand).

Always keep in mind that even in a church youth group, not everyone lives by the same standards. You still have to do your homework and know what's going on.

There might even be a time when you decide an upcoming activity is not something you want your child to attend.

Don't Pick Them Up Outside, Go In

When picking up his son from a party, my friend Anthony always made it a point to go in the house and spend a little time before he collected his son to go home. By doing that, he got to see what the party was like. He got to see what his son was having to deal with at the party, and he got to see if the information he was given before the party was correct.

"It's kind of like reviewing the films," Anthony told me as we walked through a home together. "Both my boys play football. The coaches look at the films of the teams they are about to play as well as the films of games my boys have already played. By reviewing these films the coach can help my boys play a better game of football. I want to do the same thing. I want to see the party in full swing so I can better know how to help my boys make decisions about these parties. It gives us something of value to talk about on the way home."

When you go to pick up your middle schooler from a party, go inside for a moment. See what the atmosphere is like. See what your children are dealing with. Talk to the parents. After all, it's probably been a long time since we've played Twister at a middle school party. Some things have changed.

Post-Game Discussion

Much will be said in a later chapter about the importance of talking with your child after a party, an activity, or a date. This parent-child discussion after an event becomes a golden time to open the doors to talk about not only that one event but other issues your child might be wondering about. This is a time to build your child's trust in being able to discuss even difficult issues with you, the parent. It's a time for talking and listening rather than an interrogation. Don't miss the opportunity to let your child know that you are a good listener.

One of the topics that might come up is how to interact with the opposite sex. Middle school is a good time for a child to learn about talking with and doing things with the opposite sex, but only in groups. Middle schoolers are too young to be dating in couples or even double-dating.

Many middle schoolers feel they already know how to interact with the opposite sex because they've watched how it's done on TV. But too often they quickly find out that they're wrong. Peer pressure can be very strong and a child who isn't prepared can easily be forced into some very damaging decisions.

The discussions you have with your middle schooler when they come home from a group activity help to strengthen your relationship with your child. Your child needs to be able to feel safe to ask questions, to tell you what happened. They need to know how to respond the next time something happens that makes them uncomfortable. They need to share their joys, their triumphs, the good times and the bad. This is all part of the dating process. These discussions can either distance a child from parents or start a new and better relationship with them. Be available. Listen. Accept. Guide. Don't judge.

Summary

1. Middle school is a time when young people want to begin interacting with the opposite sex. Television has made them think they know everything, but they don't.
2. Middle school is not the time to begin dating as couples or even double-dating. It's a time for group activities.

3. Parents should find out about any party or activity before giving their permission for their child to attend. They also need to teach their child how to make decisions about events.
4. Parents need to develop with their child a clear understanding of behavior, clothing, and activities that are acceptable.
5. The discussions you have with your child about what went on at a party can help to build a strong relationship with your child.
6. The social events your child attends while in middle school are a good training ground for dating in high school.

Questions to Ask Yourself

1. What are some of the activities that I as a parent believe are unacceptable for a party that my child is attending?
2. What information does my child need to give me when asking to be allowed to go to a party?
3. How can I help my child become more active in a church youth program?

Chapter 12

Location, Curfew, and Discussion

"Where do we begin?" a parent asked. "Our daughter keeps coming back from youth group saying that everyone else is 'going out.' She says she's the only one who can't 'do anything.'"

This father, whose daughter wants to know when she can start dating, should have started thinking about the basic dating issues long before this. He needs to answer the questions posed on pages 47–49: What is the right age to begin dating? How do you help your child become wise in selecting a date? What is an appropriate curfew? What are appropriate dating behaviors? These and other issues were discussed in detail. The answers to these questions change as your child gets older and gains more experience in dating. Parents need to modify their guidelines along the way. They need to let out more string, allow more freedom as a young person is able to accept more responsibility. Start now, wherever you and your child are in the dating process.

The proper age for a child to start dating is different for everyone. It depends on both the parents and the teen. It depends on how much responsibility a child can accept.

Here's a simple formula. It's not a mathematical formula. It weighs the parents' understanding of their role in the dating process and their acceptance of their child's need for more freedom with the child's own abilities.

Parental Understanding of Dating + Young Person's Abilities + Parents' Acceptance of the Emancipation Process

Parental Understanding of Dating: This formula takes the parents' understanding that dating is a process and, in a manner of speaking, "adds" it to the ability of a particular teen to handle personal responsibility. Parents need to see the importance of the dating process and accept the responsibility to guide their child throughout the process.

Young Person's Abilities: Added to this factor of parental management of the process is the teen's ability to accept responsibility, an ability that parents should have started teaching at an early age. Parents are the ones who teach their children to be accountable and responsible. These are lessons that need to be started with simple tasks, when the child is young. For example, teaching a child to get up on time in the morning lays the groundwork for the child to understand the concept of being home at a specific time when dating.

Parents' Acceptance of the Emancipation Process: The final factor in the formula is the parents' understanding and acceptance that they have to allow their child more freedom, more independence, more opportunities to make their own decisions. This is a gradual process, best started while the child is still at home, with parents available to listen, to answer questions, and to guide.

Bill and Donna raised a delightful only child named Ashley. She was everything to them and they somehow avoided the whole dating process throughout all of high school. As a family they were very active at church. They did everything together. To use Bill's words, dating for Ashley was just "unnecessary."

After Ashley graduated from high school, her parents dropped her off at a very conservative Christian college. It was close to home. Ashley could see her parents whenever she wanted.

None of that mattered. Before her freshman year was over, Ashley was far too involved with her first boyfriend. It became a very unhealthy relationship that ended abruptly after four months. The young man moved on to another socially inexperienced girl. Ashley moved back home, so distraught she dropped out of school. She never went back.

Ashley's parents, by keeping their daughter to themselves, never gave her an opportunity to learn anything about dating while still at home. Their protectiveness became a guarantee for problems. A child not only needs to learn how to interact with members of the opposite sex but also to understand what's important in a relationship. A child needs to learn how to make choices in life while still at home. A child's emancipation should begin while the child is still at home. Letting go is a slow process rather than a breaking of bonds when the child leaves home. Over-protective parents don't realize that their children need to practice flying while still near the nest.

Notice that the "formula" does not say anything about what anyone else is doing. It speaks only to the parents and their child. It doesn't even include information about what other children in the family might have done.

Your child's lament "Everyone else is dating" is not a factor. Nor should you feel pressured because your child is "continually nagging to be able to date" or because boys keep calling and you don't want your child to feel like a "weirdo."

The dating process starts with the parents and child setting parameters. The child has a clear understanding of what is acceptable and what is not, what information the parents need before they can give their approval for attending an event. Then the child has an opportunity to prove to the parents that he or she is responsible by following the rules and returning home on time. The child is given more freedom as that freedom is earned. The child learns to be responsible while away from home, learns to make decisions, learns how to handle peer pressure. And this is all regardless of what everyone else is doing.

The Right Age for Dating

There is no right age. What's right for one person will be wrong for another. In our home we selected the age of sixteen for our daughter to be able to begin double-dating. She could look forward to beginning double-dating as soon as she was sixteen. Prior to that she was involved in group dating at parties and with the church youth group. We took her to those parties and picked her up from those parties. At fifteen we let her go with other people doing the driving. If there was a problem . . . I have a beeper. She always knew that. There was no reason not to be able to reach me.

The age was different with her younger brother. Robey was allowed to double-date on special situations when he was fifteen. We always took him to the location, such as a movie theater. He knew he would not be permitted to single-date until he was sixteen. He also knew that single-dating was contingent upon how he handled his double dates. If he wasn't responsible while double-dating—didn't come home on time, became involved in unacceptable behavior—he knew he wouldn't be allowed to start single-dating until he had proven to us that he could be responsible, even if it was long after his sixteenth birthday. It was really up to him.

Relationship Vulnerable

Why were the rules different for each child? There were several reasons. The main reason was that we didn't perceive our son to be as "relationship vulnerable" as our daughter was. This doesn't mean that our son was smarter than our daughter. And it certainly didn't mean that we loved one child more than the other, so we "gave in" at fifteen instead of sixteen.

When we evaluated the situations, we saw our daughter as being more vulnerable because of the sophistication of the friends around her and the things they were permitted to do. And yes, the fact that she was a daughter played a part in that decision. Some of her girlfriends were already dating older boys, some who were even in college. That's only natural for girls to be hanging out with boys who are older and more experienced at the dating process. Our daughter's crowd was a nice crowd, but it was, at times, a group of kids who were acting older than they should have been acting. In our opinion.

Our son's closest friends were mostly his age and, being boys, not as interested in dating as girls that age are. Like most boys his age, our son's main focus was on sports. Dating was a nice extra. He did not seem as vulnerable as our daughter and so was allowed to start a little earlier.

"If I did that, I could just hear my daughter scream 'NOT FAIR,'" one father told me after a seminar. "If I don't treat them exactly the same, they attack me with the *fair* word."

Fair? What does fair have to do with it? I'm not concerned with fair. I'm concerned with ability. Though my daughter might have had to wait a year longer to begin dating, she rose to the position of having no bedtime at a much younger age than our son. Getting up in the morning and getting going are very difficult for him. As a result, he had a basic bedtime while still in high school. His sister never had a problem getting up and accomplishing the things she needed to do. She didn't need a bedtime, so didn't have one. They both understood the reasons for the difference. There was no cry of "no fair."

"That's not fair!" is a common defense relied on by American children to further their individual cause. But in this case, "not fair" is not relevant.

The Curfew

The curfew can become a constant battlefield. The child pushes for a later curfew while parents insist on an earlier time. How that gap is closed depends on how parents handle the curfew. Children gear up for battle whenever parents are inconsistent when enforcing a curfew or are unsure of what curfew is appropriate. Our kids know our weaknesses and try to exploit them. In fact, the curfew is often such a big area of difficulty between parents and child that it's a good idea to look at how parents choose to handle the conflict. We shouldn't be shocked that the kids want to change the curfew. It's in the job description of the child to push for more. "I'm big now," the child insists. "I can stay out longer." As a parent I need to know that there is going to be a push from the child. If I yell and scream and rant and rave, it's no longer the curfew that's the issue, it's our relationship. How I handle this conflict teaches my children how to handle conflict.

Parents also need to understand that what their child is asking is not necessarily what the child wants the parent to approve. Children push for the latest curfew they can possibly get. That's normal. It's healthy. It's all part of the emancipation process to push for more freedom. You'll hear arguments from your child claiming to be the "only one" who has to be in so early, the only one who has to call home if plans change. Don't give in. What is not said by many young people is that they want their parents to be their excuse for why they can't do something. It is very difficult for a teen to say to a date, "I don't really want to stay out that late" or "I want to leave before this party gets too wild." It's a lot easier to say that your parents have set eleven (or twelve) as the curfew. Understand that peer pressure to stay out late is tremendous. "You mean your parents still tell you when to be in at night?" is a taunt your children will face. Give your kids a good answer. You can even let them know that you don't mind being the heavy.

If you're having difficulty figuring out just what curfew would be appropriate for your young person to be in at night, talk to another parent. Pick someone with the same values as you have. Someone you respect. Find out how they set a curfew, what time they started at, and why. Then develop your plan, set the curfew, and be consistent. The payoff is a parent-child peace.

Event Curfew

"Where are you going?" Cynthia asked her seventeen-year-old daughter Karen when the teen asked to be allowed to go out.

"We're going to a movie and then Daniel's house after the movie. Lots of kids are going to meet there," Karen said. "What time do you want me in, Mom?"

Karen had worked her way up to a curfew of midnight, so it could have been an automatic answer—midnight. Instead, Karen's mother wanted more information. "What time is the movie over?"

"I don't even know what movie we're going to yet," Karen said, a little perturbed that her mom was asking. "Don't worry, Mom, I don't go to movies that you wouldn't approve of. I thought you said you didn't need to check on the movies I went to anymore. You said you trusted me with that!"

"Oh, I do," Cynthia said. "I wasn't questioning the movie. I was only asking about what time it ended to help me respond to your curfew question. If you don't know what time the movie is over, then be in by midnight, like always."

"You mean if I know what time the movie gets out, you'll extend my curfew?" Karen asked, quickly ditching her bad attitude as she saw a chance to stay out later than her curfew.

Karen had been double-dating since the beginning of the ninth grade. At the start of her junior year, when she began single-dating, her parents set a curfew of eleven o'clock. Karen had objected, saying she was the only one in her school with that early a curfew. But her parents wisely discussed their decision with her and consistently held to it.

Most of Karen's friends had started the same way, but some had worn down their parents with pleas, arguments, and pouting. They either got later curfews or no curfew at all. The parents who gave in to their teens' arguing did two things: They taught their children that arguing works. It has benefits. They also took away the responsibility the teens had for coming in on time. It's probably safe to assume that without any clear curfew, there were more arguments about what time the child should have returned home. Rather than working for additional dating freedom by being responsible and acting like adults, these teens were being taught to argue and manipulate their parents.

Parents who don't have clear guidelines and don't teach their child a sense of responsibility to meet those guidelines quickly become the child's enemy, the person the child has to work around. These are the children who can't wait to get away from home, who are likely to say, "Just wait until college when I will never have to face my parents when I come home at night!"

Avoid the arguments by being consistent. Avoid the yelling by staying calm. Maintain your part of the parent-child relationship by using a plan that puts the responsibility for following the plan on the child's shoulders.

With a curfew in place, a parent can choose to be flexible on the time for specific occasions. Karen's mother was preparing to be flexible. If her daughter could have given her a little more information about when the movie got out, she might have said something like, "okay, since the movie gets out at 10:40, call me when you get to Daniel's and then tonight you can stay out until 12:30."

The purpose of a curfew is to give our children some boundaries, to help them avoid situations they can't control.

Some events are special—church activities, concerts, or even school events—and these are times to show flexibility. It's not a time to redefine the curfew. These temporary changes in curfew are done for an event, because of special circumstances, not because of pleading, begging, and arguing. And the change is temporary, for a specific event.

Being inflexible on these special events shows a lack of sensitivity. Imagine a parent who refuses to let their child go to an out-of-town church event because the bus won't get back to town until midnight and the child's curfew is eleven. That would be a little ridiculous. Total rigidity and inflexibility don't teach the right lesson any more than caving in to arguments teaches children what they need to know.

It is important for the child to know that the curfew isn't to meet the parents' needs but for the child's development. The child needs to know that the parent is listening and actually has the child's welfare at heart.

Karen's mother did let her stay out later than her curfew that night. Karen liked the extension in curfew but looked a little confused. "We don't have a curfew for you just to hassle you," Karen's mother said. "We're on your side. You've been doing great at being in on time, and I thought you had earned the opportunity to stay at Daniel's a little later."

By making it clear that Karen had earned the extra time, Karen's mother was rewarding her daughter for following the rules and being responsible.

The Goal: No Curfew

Brenda started with a curfew of eleven. After being in on time for six months, her parents extended the curfew to

11:30. Her senior year the curfew was extended to midnight. On two occasions her senior year, Brenda came in late and failed to call. Both times her parents dropped her curfew back to 11:30. Brenda was upset but soon realized that being upset didn't change things. Being in on time does. Eventually her parents changed her curfew back to midnight. She had earned it.

Halfway through her senior year Brenda's parents made another change they knew they needed to do while their daughter was still at home. They announced to Brenda that she no longer had a set curfew. She could stay out late as long as she could justify the time. She had to let her parents know when she'd be home. She could not stay out all night doing nothing. Her parents made it clear that at least one of them would be up until she got home.

The "no curfew" change prompted many parent-child discussions. Brenda would push for no limit on how late she could stay out no matter what the circumstances. Her parents insisted that she had to justify her need to stay out late. This was Brenda's last year at home. In the fall she was going away to college. Her parents used that last year to help Brenda make decisions about where she was going, what she was doing, and when she'd return home. Brenda's parents wanted to prepare their daughter for the freedom she'd be enjoying on the college campus the next year.

A curfew is like a yo-yo on a string. The parent should let it out as the teen responsibly handles being in on time. When the teen can't handle the curfew, pull the yo-yo in closer. When, after a specified period of time, the teen has again functioned responsibly, let the yo-yo fly out farther on the string.

At some point before our children leave home, they need to set their own curfew. For children to be able to do that responsibly is the joint goal of the parents and the children. A teen who understands that is one who has stopped blaming and arguing and making excuses and instead attempts to act responsibly—most of the time.

Summary

1. Parents need to decide at what age their children can begin the dating process.
2. Setting a curfew depends on the child, the child's friends, and the activity.
3. The curfew should be extended when the child has been observing the curfew responsibly, over a period of months.
4. A teen needs to be taught that an extension of the curfew is directly related to how responsible the teen is in handling the current curfew.
5. The ultimate goal is for parents to be able to remove the curfew, allowing their children to decide when to come home, before the children are out on their own, in college or living in an apartment.

Questions to Ask Yourself

1. At what age do I think each of my children should begin double-dating? (The answer might be different for each teen.)
2. If my child is not yet a teen, what can I do now to teach my child the concept of accepting personal responsibility?
3. What curfew do I believe I should start with for my teen?
4. Why did I select this particular time for the curfew?

Chapter 13

The Family Interview

"I've got to tell you, I was shocked," Jack told the counselor as he described his fears. Jack and Maggie were seeing a counselor concerning a difficulty they faced with their seventeen-year-old daughter, Misty. After dating a boy for three months, Misty finally had introduced the boy to her parents, who had insisted on meeting him. Before that, whenever the boy had come to pick up Misty, she had waited by the front door and watched for her boyfriend's car, then rushed out to meet him. After Jack and Maggie met the boy, they realized they had two problems.

The first problem involved the boyfriend. Misty's boyfriend was very good looking, very persuasive, and much older than their daughter. He dressed in expensive clothes that were all black. After talking to him for a while, they realized that his philosophy of life was totally different from theirs. He was very committed to Satanism.

The second problem involved their daughter. By this time, Misty was committed to this relationship—much more committed, it turned out, than the boy was. The dating had gone on too long without any parental input or discussion. It was very difficult for the parents to break in at this point, though they tried. One day in the counselor's office, out of frustration and fear, Jack blurted out, "I can see why marriages were arranged for so many years!"

You can't go back to arranged marriages unless, of course, you want to move to another country and culture. As I think about it, that thought scares me even more than the problems we face here. I know if my father had arranged my marriage, he would have taken advantage of the opportunity to get even with me for what I had put him through during my teenage years. No, there must be a better way. And there is.

Not Arranged, But Involved

In the past, the actual marriage started with an arrangement negotiated by the parents. Today, marriage starts with a date. Date selection is the obvious time for a parent to find a way to be involved in the process. No, I'm not suggesting that parents be the ones to select the dates any more than I'm suggesting selecting a person for a child to marry, but we as parents can be involved.

How can we as parents be more involved when our children are dating? We no longer live in small communities. We rarely have the opportunity of watching other young people growing up so that we know them before they begin dating. When a son says that he is going out with so-and-so or when a daughter asks if she can go to a place with so-and-so, the names mean nothing to us.

As parents, we have three options. One option for those of us with daughters is to accept that we will never know the boys our daughters date, so why worry about it. A second is to ask our daughter about the boy who has asked her for a date and see what information she can supply before we give our permission. But collecting information about a potential date from your teen is very unproductive. The information isn't reliable. If a girl wants to go out with the boy (and I'm assuming she wouldn't be asking if she didn't want to go), she isn't likely to give parents any negative facts.

That's what Misty did. Remember the girl who didn't introduce her boyfriend to her parents until after she'd been going out with him for three months? Her parents, Jack and Maggie, had asked their daughter about the boy she was dating. Misty never lied. She just chose to give her parents the good parts of the information. She knew the young man was inappropriate for her, but she was so enamored with him that she withheld the information her parents really needed.

Sometimes our teens won't even have the information they need. A boy asks a girl out, and the girl really wants to go to the particular event. She's seen him at school, but doesn't know anything about him other than he does play a sport.

The third and only successful option is for parents to ask the potential date for information. Without a doubt, a parent needs to interview each potential date.

"You're not serious!" fourteen-year-old Hannah said in astonishment. Her father had just told her he intended to meet every boy before she went out on a date with him.

"What do you mean 'meet him'?" Hannah cried. "Are you going to ask him questions? Interrogate him? What would you ask him?"

Hannah was only fourteen and not yet dating. She and her parents were sitting at the kitchen table, talking about dating and at what age Hannah could start dating. Hannah was already interested in boys and had asked once again when she could think about going out on a date. This part of the dating process—having her parents meet every boy— had until then gone unmentioned.

Hannah looked stricken. "I guess I don't need to ask you anymore when I can date. I'll never have any dates anyway!"

Why an Interview?

The reaction at our house was similar. The first thing our daughter wanted to know when she heard we'd insist on meeting every date before she went out was "why?"

"Nobody else does this! Why do we have to?" Torrey wanted to know. "Why do we have to have a boy over to talk to you before I can go out with him? Dad, I'll never get a date."

Actually there were other parents who wanted to meet their daughters' dates before the daughter could go out. We knew it. Torrey found out later that we weren't so different from other parents. She was also wrong about never getting asked for a date after guys found out they had to come over first and meet us. We wanted our daughter to know that she was special to us and that the privilege of taking her on a date was exactly that—a privilege. "Oh, Dad," she said, "that's not really true."

"To me it's very true," I said. "Torrey, let me see if I can explain how I feel about this. If a boy I'd never met called me at home on a Tuesday night and asked if he could borrow my car to go to a movie, what do you think I would say? Mind you now, I've never met him. Do you think that I would loan him my car for the evening? I don't think so! Do you think I consider my car, a possession, more precious to me than you are?" I looked at my daughter for some kind of response and then went on. "If you are more precious to me than anything, why would I send you out on a date with a boy I've never met? I think that would be stupid on my part."

Parents need to meet the boys their daughter dates not only because of how much they love her but also to let each boy know that fact. The boy needs to realize that the family of the girl he's taking out on a date holds her in very high regard. He needs to see that she is precious to her family. Many boys today grow up with a concept (conscious or subconscious) that girls are to be used. Movies, music, and even talk in their own homes portray women as something to be used for sexual pleasure and little more.

One girl, a junior in high school, came home from her first date in tears. Her parents calmed her down, and she was able to tell them what had happened. The parents, knowing the boy went to the same Christian school as their daughter, had been impressed when he picked their daughter up for the date with flowers in hand. He had taken her to a nice restaurant for dinner and then to a friend's house for a party. At the party the boy suggested that they go into the backyard to sit and talk. She agreed. But after getting to the backyard he immediately attempted to kiss her and put his hand in her blouse. When she protested, he acted shocked. The girl asked to be taken home and the boy acted even more shocked, but he agreed and they left the party. It was a very quiet drive home. As they pulled up to her house, the boy finally said, "I certainly expected more after all the money I spent on you."

That young man had expectations about what they each wanted from the date. He knew girls liked flowers, dinner at a fancy restaurant. But he also was somehow taught that girls were there to please boys, even wanted or at least expected to please the boys who spent money on them.

How could meeting the parents have changed that situation? Nothing could guard against that situation. But meeting the parents would have helped the boy connect the girl to a family. She wasn't just a girl alone; there were people at home who loved her, a family with a philosophy of life that women are to be treated like ladies. Spending a few moments to get to know a young man helps him get to know who the family is rather than just what his potential date looks like. It helps get deeper than the physical.

The third reason to meet the boy is to meet the boy. The meeting provides an opportunity to find out who the boy is, where he goes to church, and what he believes. Those aren't awkward questions if they're handled in a friendly, non-intimidating manner. Several things are accomplished with this line of discussion. Not only does it allow the parents and the young man to jump to a deeper level of discussion, it also sets the stage for the boy and girl to have that kind of discussion.

"Dad," Lana said to her father, "I never expected this to happen, but after you talked to Ryan on Sunday afternoon and asked him about what he believed, it opened the door for us to have a talk about God. When he called me tonight he finally said, 'Wow, your dad is really cool. I've never even talked to my own dad about stuff like that. He really cares about you. But you know what, I felt like he even cared about me.' From there we went on to talk about what we believe. It was great!"

It's often difficult for young people to get past the small talk or the talk about music and movies to get on to talking about things that are important to them, like their faith. With a parent opening the door to such a conversation during the meeting, it makes it easier for the teens to start into that kind of discussion.

The meeting between parent and date accomplishes many things. It helps the girl and boy both come to realize how precious the family considers their teen to be. The meeting helps the potential date know who the family is, that the teen they are going out with is connected to a family. This is not just an individual they are going out with. The time a parent spends with a daughter's date, for example, helps the date know what the family's philosophy of life is. It also helps the family begin to know something about the boy their daughter is dating. Though I have heard that many boys initially feared this meeting, I have also heard that they were grateful for it later on. It helped them feel more comfortable with the whole family rather than feeling like an unwanted intruder. This meeting should be fun.

Meeting a Son's Date

What about a son? The logistics make it a little more difficult for parents to meet a son's date. Is such a meeting important? Yes, it is every bit as important, though it probably needs to be handled differently. Even though a son is somewhat more in control of deciding which girls to date (or does he just think he's in control?), it is important for parents to have an opportunity to meet the girl. Meeting the girl during the first date by having her over to the house is ideal. That way she can get to know the family at the beginning.

Seeing and talking to a son's date give parents a good indication of what they might have to deal with concerning this specific girl. One father said he called his son on the car phone to ask him to stop by the house before he took his date to a party. The son picked up his date, who did not realize she would be seeing his parents before making her grand entrance at the party. Both parents and date were shocked. When the boy pulled up at his house and said, "Come on in for a second," his date responded, "But I'm not dressed to see your parents." When she did come in, the parents were shocked to see how provocatively she was dressed (or should I say not dressed?). This prompted the parents to have a long talk with their son later on that weekend.

Yes, parents should meet the girls that their sons are dating. It is equally important for the son's date to understand the philosophy of life the family is trying to live by. That makes it easier for the son to talk to a girl about who he is and what his standards are. If parents don't set the standards, their son could be left to fend for himself in a very provocative environment.

How to Handle the Interview

The interview, or meeting, should be light and fun. It is best done in the home rather than during an activity outside the home. It doesn't need to be long, but it does need to build a relationship with your child's date. Let your child's date get to know you a little bit, just don't bore them with a lot of talk about yourself. And don't make the meeting an interrogation.

Guy used his home to meet the guys who asked his daughters out. When a boy would ask one of his daughters for a date, at school or over the phone, the daughter would say that she wasn't permitted to go out with anyone her father hadn't met. Immediately, as father and daughter had rehearsed, the daughter would say, "Why don't you come over Sunday afternoon after church? You could come over for lunch or come later and even go to church with us at six if you want."

Obviously a lot of information passes hands with that invitation. The daughter tells the would-be suitor that she can't go out on a date until he has met her dad. She also indicates that she would like to go out with him by immediately offering him a time to come by to meet her father. The boy is also made aware of the fact that the family goes to church.

When a boy comes by the house in the evening or on a Sunday afternoon, the father-boy meeting should be fun and easy. In fact, the boy should be put at ease by being in a situation where he is comfortable. That might be sitting on the patio with other family members so the meeting is very conversational. It might mean sitting in the living room for a while, just the girl's father and the boy.

The conversation could begin with, "Glen, I'm Mr. Sisson, Linda's father. She's still upstairs and will be down in a minute. Come sit down in the living room while you wait. I'm glad to have this opportunity to meet you. You are a friend of Linda's from school? Do you have classes together?"

From there ask about the boy's family while you tell him about yours. Make the conversation easy by sharing similar things or experiences about both families. Ask where he goes to church and tell him where you go to church. Tell the boy about your personal and family faith. "I'm glad to hear that you go to church. I've heard a lot of good things about your church, Glen. We have a strong commitment to Christ here. In fact we want to please Christ with everything we do as a family or as individual family members."

At this point a dad will have to decide if he feels comfortable asking the boy if he has ever received Christ himself, personally. Sometimes it's appropriate and sometimes it's a little mechanical and intense. The goal here is not to make the boy pass out but to help the boy feel comfortable and get to know who the family is and what they stand for.

"What do you do if the boy indicates that he does not believe as you do?" one parent asked. "Do you end the conversation and tell him he can't go out with your daughter right then and there?"

Everyone has to decide the next step for themselves. As for me, rather than making the announcement to the boy, I'd respect my daughter enough to discuss it with her. The discussion with the boy has helped him understand that there are differences in our philosophies of life. I might be the first Christian he has met. I want to be available to minister to him rather than send him away feeling as if I judged him.

"Does that mean that you would let your daughter go out with a boy who was not a Christian?" In my opinion, and let me stress that it is my opinion, I would rather spend the time discussing this with my daughter. There's a bigger picture here. One day every daughter will be sitting away from home, perhaps on a college campus, without a dad to do the interview of a potential date. It is more productive to discuss any problems with your daughter and help her come to a determination as to what she should do after she has heard the facts.

If the boy is not a Christian, it would seem to make more sense to invite him back to your home or to go to church with you. Pursue the spiritual condition of the boy and slow down the dating process. One of two things will probably happen. Either the boy will decide that this is more than he bargained for and move on, or he will become interested in the whole family and become a Christian, as I did.

No plan is foolproof, or should I say no plan puts a parent in total "control" of the dating process. What a parent is doing here is setting the stage for the dating process to be most likely to succeed. Meeting the parents is an opportunity for the young man, or the young woman, to understand who the family is and what they stand for.

Pass the Baton

My friend John Ream would begin his meeting with suitors who came to pick up one of his daughters with a compliment, then spell out just what he expected. He'd say, "I'm glad to see your good taste. We consider our daughter to be like a very special pearl. A pearl to be cherished and protected.

"If there was a fire in our home, I would have a special role as the man. I would see to it that I was the last one out of the house. I would never consider leaving this house until I was sure my wife and daughters were safely out of the house. Their safety and security are my responsibility.

"As you take our daughter out on a date, I temporarily pass that responsibility on to you. You are now responsible for her safety. I would never do anything that would make her feel like she wasn't in a safe place or a safe situation. I would never let her feel frightened. I pass the baton of her safety into your hands."

Results of the Interview

Parents who are interested enough to get involved in a meeting process show their teens that they are really loved. "I'm not doing this just to hassle you, Honey. To tell you the truth, I'm a little nervous about the whole meeting thing myself. I'm going to the trouble to do this because I love you and think this is real important."

The results of the meeting offer a great opportunity for parents and child to together process impressions and any concerns regarding the date. Parents need to be very careful not to voice their thoughts in a judgmental way. In fact, the most productive way is to offer information and ask what your child thinks. Offer your own conclusions when asked, and they are more likely to be heard, rather than dismissed. The most significant part of the whole meeting process happens afterward, when parents and child take the time to discuss the results of the meeting. The less dogmatic a parent is, the more likely the child will learn how to weigh information to recognize any potential problems. It's important to remember that your children will eventually be away from home and have to perform their own interviews. They should not be told *what* to think. They should be taught *how* to think.

The meeting itself should be fun, not intense. Take the time to be easy rather than using the time to fire off questions at a date as if you're both in an interrogation room. One boy brought a friend with him when he went to a girl's house to meet her parents. Because he was a little nervous, he brought some support. The conversation between the parent and the two boys turned out to be informative for both boys and a lot of laughs. Having another young man there lightened up the whole scene. Later on that afternoon, when the daughter and the two young men were sitting out on the back patio, the friend said to the girl, "Wow, your family is great. You all really care about each other, don't you." He wasn't the one feeling under pressure, so he could see the scene for what it really was.

"You all really care about each other, don't you." Mission accomplished!

Summary

1. Decide ahead of time that your daughter, or son, is important enough to you for you to meet the person who wants to go out on a date with them.
2. Establish the concept of meeting dates with your child before dating begins so that your child is prepared for it.
3. Make the mechanics of the meeting easy. Give your child suggestions on how to set it up. Show that you really are on your child's side.
4. Make the meeting informative for your child's date as well as for you.
5. Have fun with the meeting and then take the time to discuss the results of the meeting with your child.

Questions to Ask Yourself

1. How can I help my daughter understand the value of this pre-date meeting process?
2. When is the best time to meet a potential date in my home?
3. What is the best way for me to meet a girl my son would like to take out?
4. What will I tell my teen is the reason for this meeting?

Chapter 14

The Double Date

"You mean if we don't find someone else to go to the movies with, we can't go? We just can't go alone?" Mark said to his parents in total exasperation.

"Mark, you act like this is all new to you," his mother said. "This is the way it's been since you started dating. You know that you can't go out on a date unless there's another couple."

Parents should never be surprised or confused at their teen's ongoing attempts to accelerate the process of dating. Mark's parents had already established that during this particular time he was only permitted to double-date. If his mother hadn't known why the process of dating was to be started with double-dating, this might have been the day she caved in. Her son, whom she loved, was caught in a bind. He had asked a girl to go to the movies and, in his excitement, forgot about asking another couple. Mark was trying to turn his problem into his mother's problem. But she put it right back on his shoulders. She did it because she understood the value of being consistent and staying with the dating plan.

The reason for starting the dating process with four going on the date rather than just two is obvious. The intimacy that is possible for a boy and a girl alone on a date puts them in a very vulnerable position. During a date, the two are unaccountable to anyone. Having another couple along takes away some of that freedom and helps create more of an accountability. There is also strength in numbers, although that strength can sometimes work against you.

The issue of double-dating is more than simply having four people on a date. It is also important to know who the other couple is, what their standards are. Holly arranged for another couple to go along when she went out with Jeff. But Holly, a tenth grader, wasn't prepared to deal with the pressure that was brought on by the other couple.

Holly had met Jeff at church. He was one of the young men from the local college who attended their church. They noticed each other and finally Jeff asked Holly to go out on a date. She told him she couldn't go out alone with anybody, that it had to be a double date. "No problem," he said. He'd bring his roommate George and George's girlfriend.

That met the requirements for a double date, but it didn't help the situation. Holly didn't know that Jeff and the other couple were looking forward to getting some pizza and then going to an abandoned road outside of town to park. In this case, double-dating only added to the pressure. Holly suddenly understood that she had to be more careful when picking the other couple for a double date.

Double-Date with Like-Minded Friends

Holly told her parents what had happened, which gave her father an opportunity to discuss the importance of picking the right couple, not accepting just anyone. "That's where we made our mistake on your date with Jeff. We just filled the seat with anyone we could find. We met the requirement, but not the need," he said. "And they weren't mature enough to help you when you needed help. Needless to say, I'm proud of the way you handled yourself with Jeff. All by yourself, you pulled yourself out of a bad situation."

Holly understood, probably for the first time, that her parents' requirement that she go out only on double dates was not just to hassle her. It was for her own benefit. It was a safety factor.

One way to explain the need for double-dating to your teen is to compare it to learning to drive. The beginning driver needs someone in the front seat, right next to them, who can take over the driving or help out if necessary. The young person does the driving, but the driving instructor is ready to help out if there's a problem. The beginning driver can count on the driving instructor to be there, to be a backup.

Double-dating can provide the same kind of backup. You have another person along in case you need some backup to get out of a difficult situation. Just as you pick a driving instructor who is a good driver, you pick someone for a double date who has the same values as you do, who will back you up when you say "no." Or "I want to go home now."

Teens don't appreciate the double date rule until they need it, until they're being forced to do something that they really don't want to do. Peer pressure to act "adult" is great, especially on a date when you're away from the supervision of parents. What the right double date can do is get some of that peer pressure working for the teen who is saying "no." Make sure your teens understand how important it is to pick another couple for double-dating who believe as they do. Then if one person starts to get out of line, the others are there to help out, to keep the situation from going bad.

Double-dating also helps to make the date more of an activity rather than an intimate relationship. When there are four, or more, everyone puts on a public face, doing things together, talking together, having fun together. Two alone are more prone toward experimenting with this new area of intimacy. Think about what married couples tend to do when they go out on a date. They're not going out for intimacy. They're looking for entertainment and, to add to the fun of the evening, they invite another couple to go along. They invite someone who can help carry the evening, who contributes to the enjoyment. For many, especially those who are not very adept at communication, it helps to make the event more enjoyable.

In reality, no one, teen or adult, knows what to expect from the dating process. Several years ago, in the movie *Sleepless in Seattle*, Tom Hanks, a widower, finds himself "back in the saddle again," as he put it—once again attempting to figure out dating. Much of the humor of the movie is built around his fear and tentativeness about dating. If the Tom Hanks character, who has already been married once, is nervous about dating, how much more tense will our teens be?

The questions our teens will have about dates are unending. What to do? How to please? What to say? Where can we go? The pressure of the date can be overwhelming, especially when the teen is going out with a person who is more experienced at dating. The fears and the pressures to perform well are too overwhelming for a young teen to take on alone. Having a good friend along is not only a safety factor but can make the date a lot more fun.

Making It Happen

Our teens may understand our rules—and even agree with them—but not know how to make it all work. Lindie, who had finally reached the age for double-dating, thought the whole dating process was too complicated with all the rules her parents had imposed. "How will I be able to make it all happen? It's hard enough to get a date without having to find another couple to go with you," she said to her dad one day. "And you have to meet them all first. How can I make all that happen?"

Lindie's dad listened as his daughter spilled out her frustration. Her frustration wasn't so much with the plan as it was with making it work. "What if I did this," he said.

"During the process of meeting the boy, I'll tell him that that's the rule, that you have to double-date. It'll take all the pressure off of you and put it on us. Don't worry. I won't embarrass you."

"What will you say?" Lindie said.

"I'll say something like, 'I don't know if Lindie had a chance to tell you, but we're kind of old-fashioned when it comes to dating. Well, I guess you do know we're old-fashioned, since we wanted to meet you. For now, when Lindie goes out on dates, we want them to be double dates. And to tell you the truth, if possible we'd like to know the other boy and girl.' Would something like that help?"

"Dad, that's okay, but if you could leave out the last part about wanting to know the other boy and girl, it would be better. That sounds so controlling. Like you're going to put a homing device on me next."

The important thing was not that Lindie and her parents came up with the perfect way to make this double-dating happen. What was most important was that Lindie learned from their discussion that her parents wanted to make the process as easy as possible for her. With the dating plan in place, her parents jumped on her side to help her make it happen in the most comfortable way possible. Parents can offer suggestions and be available for ongoing explanations.

Some overly controlling parents need to check their motives for establishing dating procedures. Is it to make it difficult for their teen to get a date? Are they imposing controls and limits without any reason other than to stop their teen from socializing with the opposite sex? Or are they trying to help the teen succeed at dating? Are they preparing their children for the dating world after high school, when their children are no longer in their home?

A double date should give your child support from a friend when they find themselves in unfriendly territory. There is strength in sticking together. A double date is a tool to have a friend along, someone to count on in time of trouble.

Summary

1. Double-dating is a great way to begin practicing the process of dating. It's the next logical step after group activity dating.
2. Double-dating supplies the teen with a friend to count on if a particular dating situation becomes uncomfortable.
3. Double-dating can provide safety in numbers if the other couple includes a like-minded friend. If not, it can just add to peer pressure.
4. Parents need to help their child to figure out how to present the rule of double-dating to a prospective date.

Questions to Ask Yourself

1. Why is double-dating important to me as a teaching parent? How can I make my child understand why it is a necessary part of the dating process without turning the rule into a legalistic hassle for my child?
2. How can I help my child to know how to pick the right couple to go out with on a double date?
3. In what way can I make it easier for my children to present my double-date "rule" to their friends?

Chapter 15

And Finally, the Date

Your teen will be pushing for the next step—a real date without another couple along. Like all other steps in the dating process, this step is earned.

How can you tell if your child is ready for single-dating? A teen who has acted responsibly for a period of time on double dates has earned the right to take the next step. But there's another very important factor to consider. Make sure your child actually wants to go out alone on a date. Some don't, even though they're asking to be allowed to go. Too often kids get caught up in what everyone else is doing and they can get pushed into something before they're ready.

That's what almost happened to Nancy. All her friends were going to a big formal dance and they were pushing her to go. One of the boys in their crowd was going to call her. Her friends, who had been asked to find out if she'd go, kept asking, "Will you go?" Nancy was excited about going but also feeling something else—almost a dread. She wanted to go, but . . . Every time the phone rang, she avoided answering it. She didn't understand why everyone else was so excited about the dance. Why wasn't she?

One night after dinner, while doing dishes, Nancy finally told her mother that she might get invited to go to the dance. That her friends said Jimmy Frasier was going to ask her. "Can I go, Mom?"

Nancy was sixteen and had double-dated a few times. But most of the time she stuck more with a group, where boys and girls did things together without pairing off.

"Do you want to go?" her mother asked.

"Of course I want to go. Everybody is going," Nancy said.

"Well, then let's talk about what you'll be doing. What we'll have to buy so you can go," her mother said.

As they talked, Nancy's mother got the distinct impression that her daughter was reluctant to go to the dance. She didn't seem comfortable with the idea of spending a whole evening with one boy, all dressed up, dancing. The big question was: Was Nancy asking to go just because her friends were going and she'd feel odd if she didn't?

Parents need to be able to hear more than just what their child is saying; they need to be able to hear what the child is not saying. In Nancy's case, she still wasn't comfortable with the whole dating thing. It's not what she wanted to do at this particular time in her life. No major reason. To her, the idea of a formal dance just wasn't fun. She was having too much fun with other things, playing basketball and baseball, playing in the band, and going skiing— doing things as part of a group. But more important, she didn't like any particular boy enough to want to go out with him on a date. It's not that she didn't like the boy who was going to call. She did. They were friends. But ...

When Nancy's mother again asked if she really wanted to go, Nancy finally said, "I think so."

Nancy's mother realized then that her daughter was not ready to go and shouldn't. She just had to find a way to explain this to Nancy and help her to know that it was okay not to go. She didn't have to follow the crowd. She could make her own decision.

It's a lot like swimming in the ocean. Kids have fun playing around, swimming in the deeper water, farther from shore. Then they get caught on a wave that's coming in to the beach. It's scary. It's not fun. They don't want to be there. They'd rather be in the calm waters farther out. But they don't know how to get off the rushing wave. And finally they can't get off. They have to go wherever the wave takes them.

Nancy didn't go to the formal dance that year. The boy did call. And after hearing her reason for not wanting to go, he said he didn't much like dances either and asked if she'd like to go to a movie instead. They did.

How do you tell if your child is ready for single-dating? Talk with your child, especially after a double date. Listen. Get a feel for the direction the relationship is going as well as how your child is feeling about the whole idea of dating. Is your child getting too serious about someone? Too soon? Is your child able to handle unacceptable issues while on a date? Has your child shown responsible behavior? But most importantly, is your child pushing for single-dating? Or being pushed by others? Does your child feel ready or is your child caught on a wave and doesn't know how to get off?

Barbara kept pushing her parents to let her go out with her boyfriend alone, without having another couple along. She was tired of all the hassle, never knowing if Greg would be able to find another guy for a double date. She dreamed about how nice it would be to be alone with Greg. Her parents finally agreed.

On their first real date—alone—to a party, Greg dropped Barbara off in front of the house, then went to park the car. She was standing on the porch, waiting for him, watching other kids going in, when she smelled marijuana. One of the guys standing just inside the door had a joint in his hand.

Barbara knew she shouldn't stay. But what could she do? What would Greg want to do? Not everyone would be smoking pot. Maybe they could just be careful.

"What's the matter?" Greg asked as he joined her on the porch.

"I don't think we should be here," Barbara said. "I smell pot."

Just then the door opened again and Greg, too, recognized the familiar odor. "What do you want to do?" he asked.

"I'd rather go to a movie," Barbara said.

They both called their parents to tell them about the change in plans. They heard the next day in school that the party had gotten pretty rowdy and neighbors had called the police.

Barbara's parents heard about the party from some other parents whose kids had stayed. They told their daughter how proud they were of the decision she and Greg had made to avoid the problem. That's when Barbara admitted that the family practice sessions on handling difficult situations had paid off. "I used to feel kind of silly when you and dad would make me practice what I'd say, but it sure made it a lot easier. Not only did I know I shouldn't be there when I smelled that pot, the words I'd need to say all came rushing back to me. I knew what to do and what to say."

Barbara's parents had given her just what she needed to handle the situation. Not only did she know the right thing to do—and what would be all wrong—but she knew an alternative. She knew what to say. She didn't have to wonder.

A strange thing happens as teens are given more freedom in dating. They often revert back to a requirement that's already been lifted. When Becky's parents told her that she had "graduated" and was no longer limited to double dates, Becky was excited about the change but still went out on double dates quite often. She seemed to have more fun with another couple along than she did when she went out alone with a boy. She was just more comfortable on a double date.

Her parents didn't say anything about the continuation of double-dating. They were pleased. Relieved. The safety factor was still in place. But now the choice was being made by their daughter. The double date was no longer required by her parents.

"Remember when Becky was learning to swim?" her dad said to her mother one night. "Remember how she hated wearing the water wings in the pool? Said it made her feel like a baby."

"Oh, yes, and I remember how hard she worked to be able to tread water for the span of time you required so she wouldn't have to wear them," her mother replied. "Remember that day when she finally could? Didn't she even set a timer by the pool?"

"She sure did. And she made it. Do you remember what she did after that?"

"No, what?"

"Every so often she'd put on her water wings even though she didn't need to wear them anymore. I guess she was just more comfortable with them on," her father said. "And then it was her choice."

For Becky, the double dates were like her old water wings in the pool. They both made her feel more comfortable. Double-dating is good practice for preparing a teen to take the next step—single-dating. But the teen needs to understand that double-dating isn't just a parental requirement. It's fun.

Turning Down a Date

"Dad, did you ever have a girl ask you to go to something with her, and you really wanted to go to that particular thing ... but you didn't want to go with her? Dad?"

Jeremy's dad put down the sports section and looked up at his son. "What's the matter?"

"Diane Smith, at school, has invited me to be her date at the Spring Festival at Bayside Country Club. I'd really like to go ... but not with her. And I think another girl might ask me," Jeremy said. "What do you do when someone asks you on a date and you don't want to go out with them?"

Jeremy's dilemma is usually on the other foot. Girls usually have to decide what to do in this kind of situation. There are several things to consider, no matter which gender is being asked. Do you have to accept the invitation from the first person who asks? Or not go? Is it okay to turn someone down for a date to a particular event and then go with someone else who asks later on?

What is appropriate? What's the right thing to do? Each parent will want to answer those particular questions in their own way. It's important to remind your child that the feelings of another person are involved. But saying yes to the first person who asks isn't necessarily the right answer. If Jeremy turns down Diane, who asked him first, then accepts an invitation from another girl, who asks later, Diane's feelings will be hurt. What's being kind in that situation? What's not kind? Would Jeremy be considered self-centered if he turned down Diane and went with someone else? Should he not go at all, even if someone he wants to go with asks him later?

In order to be polite, do you have to say "yes"? Is being polite the most important consideration? Some young people believe you're stuck—unless you want to be rude or lie about what you're doing that night.

What would you do?

It was 1968. Rosemary was a freshman on our campus . . . and beautiful. Lots of guys wanted a date with her, including me. I called to ask her to a party, explaining that I was the guy who had talked to her after French class. I will never forget her answer. I don't remember her exact words, but this is very close to what she said.

"Oh, hi. You don't have to remind me. I remember talking to you today. You're a friend of Tom's."

I was on a roll. She sounded so absolutely positive, I knew I would have a date. With her. So I went for it. "A bunch of us are getting together Friday night after the game for a party. Would you like to go with me?"

Nothing could have prepared me for her response. Nothing.

"Thanks for thinking about me," she said. "As a matter of fact I asked Tom about you today when he was here visiting Peggy. He said you were a great guy, but that you and I were in two different worlds. He didn't mean that as a negative about you. In fact, it was probably a little bit of a statement about how 'overly conservative,' as he put it, I am. You see, I've made a decision not to go out with anyone who isn't a born-again Christian. Not because of them, you understand, but because of me. I'm just not into drinking and all the stuff that goes with it. I'm honored that you would invite me to the party, but I just can't go. I will say this, though. I'd like to invite you to go to church with us this Sunday."

I stood in the phone booth trying to get some air. I mumbled something and hung up. That was not what I had expected. Never had I heard someone so confident in what they believed. She had turned me down. Yet I walked away from that phone call feeling somehow honored to be turned down. I didn't feel rejected. Actually, I felt she had rejected herself from the party. I felt okay about being turned down, but not yet okay enough to go with her to church.

That fall, I invited Rosemary to several other events—and got turned down and invited to church each time. On the sixth or seventh try, I finally gave in and went to church. That was the beginning of a great quest for me.

Rosemary's response to being asked out on a date by a person she really didn't want to go out with was a carefully rehearsed answer. Only later did I find out that she was very nervous during our phone calls. She never sounded nervous. She immediately took gentle control of the conversation. She had already thought through (and practiced) the way she was going to answer a request for a date from someone who wasn't a Christian. Her speech, though practiced, made me *feel* as if I really understood why we couldn't go out, even though at first I didn't.

Parents need to help their teens figure out an appropriate response to an inappropriate request. Acting it out with your child sounds silly, but it can be helpful when the actual test comes. I never had any idea that Rosemary wasn't as confident as her rehearsed speech made her sound.

Having a proper response ready helps your child avoid going out with a person they don't want to go out with and be able to do it without insulting or hurting that person. The first question the teen has to answer is, "Why don't I want to go out with this particular person?" The answer will give the teen the beginnings of the response needed when the phone rings.

Heather knew she was about to be asked out by a boy who was a very strong Christian. The problem was that Heather wasn't interested in him. "Does the fact that he is actually a Christian mean that I can't turn him down for a date?" she asked her father.

"No, you aren't required to go out with anyone just because they fulfill the number-one thing on your list. You just have to think about how you're going to say no. You could avoid him—"

"That's impossible, Dad," Heather cut in. "We're both on youth group council together."

"Then when he asks, think of how to tell him that you enjoy him as a friend, and that you don't think it would be good for the two of you to go out."

"Oh, that sounds like it would be so hard to do," Heather said. "I don't want to hurt his feelings. I still want to be his friend."

"The other approach," her father pointed out, "is to go out with him once and hurt his feelings even more when you turn him down the next time. Then you really will lose him as a friend."

Difficult Confrontations

As hard as it sounds to tell someone who has just asked you out on a date that you can't go, teens need to be prepared for even more difficult situations when dating. And parents can help by discussing these situations ahead of time, helping their children formulate responses, and reminding them of the importance of their commitment to purity. Your teenager needs to know how to say no.

Gone are the days when it was considered the girl's role to be strong and keep a boy from going too far on a date, from becoming sexually active. In today's culture, some girls have grown up thinking that the way you express love is by giving your body. And boys are made to feel that it wouldn't be macho to walk away from a sexual opportunity on a date. Our teenagers are fighting peer pressure and raging biology. They're seeing sex, or the representation of sex, in the movies and on TV. It's portrayed as the thing to do, even on a first date. No big deal. Time was when parents taught their girls not to kiss on a first date. A boy might think she was too easy.

Today's parents need to be talking to both their boys and their girls about taking a stand, about making a commitment to purity. They need to emphasize not only the importance of saving themselves as a gift for their future spouse, but the dangers they face if they don't, the diseases—AIDS, gonorrhea, syphillis, and other sexually transmitted diseases—that can change their life forever, even prove fatal.

It's vital for parents to explain to a child how quickly a poor decision, a mistake, can turn to disaster. I will never forget reading an article about the movie *Fatal Attraction*. The man in the movie got into an extra-marital relationship very quickly, in an hour or so, probably without thinking much about the consequences. The next thing he knew he had compromised all his standards and jeopardized his marriage. He couldn't undo what he had done.

Our children need to be prepared for the kinds of situations that they will face while dating. Parents must give their teens all the weapons possible. They must help their teens know where not to be on a date, what not to do. They need to know the very real dangers they face. Teens need help in figuring out ahead of time what to say so there's no hesitation. They need to know what is the right thing to do. But it's really up to the teen to decide to do the right thing, to say no when necessary. When parents have done their job, preparing their teens, a child won't have to say, "It caught me off guard! I just didn't know what to say."

Dating can be a great adventure for a young person who knows what to expect, who feels confident, and who knows how to respond to potentially uncomfortable or dangerous situations. It's the unexpected that can make dating a tense and difficult time for a teen. Help your children get ready for dating. Prepare them. You'll be helping them to stay safe and to win at the dating game.

Summary

1. One of the most difficult parts about dating is dealing with the unknown. Parents can help by providing information, by walking their teens through some of those unknowns.
2. Parents can help their teen think through how to turn down a date by first understanding why the date isn't appropriate.
3. Practicing how to deal with a request for a date that is either inappropriate or from a person they just don't want to go out with gives a teen a feeling of confidence.

4. Knowing how to handle difficult situations that might come up on dates starts with being aware of what might happen, then figuring out what you would do if faced with the situation.

Questions to Ask Yourself

1. How and when will I know that my child is ready for single-dating?
2. What do I think are appropriate reasons to turn down a person who is asking for a date? (You can't help your child answer that question until you think about the dilemma yourself.)
3. How can I help my child prepare responses to difficult situations that might occur on a date? What kinds of situations could occur?
4. When is a good time to have these somewhat difficult discussions with my child?

Chapter 16

Post-Game Discussion

"Who does your Donny talk to," Rosemary asked a couple sitting across from us at dinner, "when he comes in from a date?"

"He really doesn't talk to either of us. He just comes in, sticks his head in our bedroom door, and says good night. That's really the extent of it."

Rosemary and I have found that our very best time of communication about what's going on in the lives of our children is right after they come in from a date. While the exciting experience of a date is still fresh, it's important for your teen to have someone to talk to about what went on. It's very interesting that teens will usually pick the person and the place. If a parent isn't readily available to listen, many teens, especially girls, will go so far as to work up a phone signal with a friend so they can call and talk late at night. Right after a date.

This post-date discussion can be one of the most productive and teachable moments in the parent-child relationship. However, for this to happen, there are some very significant things that need to take place.

Be Available

Both parents are not needed for this post-date discussion time. In fact, two parents might be overwhelming. But no matter how late the hour might be, it is very important that one parent is still up and awake enough for the young person to be able to feel comfortable talking about the evening's events. One parent must decide that staying up is their job.

How do you decide which one should stay up for talking? That's actually a very easy decision. Parents don't need to make it. Your teen usually makes it for you. Your teen will most likely select which parent he or she wants to communicate with. Kids pick the parent who is the best listener and the least judgmental.

In our home my daughter, Torrey, made it very clear which one of us she wanted to talk to. Early on, she went so far as to seek her mother out after a date or an activity. She would come in from a youth group event at church when she was only fourteen and would want to talk to Rosemary about something that happened that night. Even if the happening wasn't significant, she still wanted to talk about it. Once Torrey had selected her mother, Rosemary made the commitment to be up and ready to listen each and every night Torrey came in.

"Why didn't she choose me?" I remember asking Rosemary one night. My feelings were a little hurt.

"Because you sometimes don't let her finish her sentences, Bob. She initially just wants to talk. She's using me to bounce her evening off of. Besides, you've made so many jokes about not ever letting her get married, that she'll have to live here forever, she just might be afraid of hurting your feelings if she says she really likes a certain boy. She knows you're kidding, but ..."

Our children do pick the parent who is the better listener. But sometimes, in other ways, they let the other parent in on what's going on. During Torrey's senior year, she did something that showed I could listen if I wanted to, but please don't interrupt. She changed the location of many of their conversations. Instead of sitting down in the family room curled up in a chair, as they had been doing, mother and daughter got into their pajamas and Torrey would sit on the foot of the bed, talking. The lights would be out. I was there, half asleep. She knew I might be awake enough to listen, but if they were noisy enough to wake me and I asked a question, they apologized for waking me and moved downstairs. So that I could get some sleep, they said. Again, Torrey wanted me to hear, she just didn't want my judgments.

"But my teen just isn't a night person," a mother said in frustration. "Billy comes in from a date, says good night, and he's asleep before his head hits the pillow. I can't get him to talk to me at night."

Do it the next day, whenever it works for you and your teen. Understand that your child does need you to listen, to hear about what's going on, to know that you care and can serve as a cheering section, an adviser, a friend. Don't just say, "It's time to talk." Develop the habit of a feedback time with each of your children. For our son, who isn't a night person or a morning person, we had to work at finding a good time. We couldn't start firing questions the next morning. He didn't want to talk then. He would talk later in the day with either his mother or me, whoever had the time to listen. It didn't seem to matter which one. Many talks took place in the car, when it was just two of us. Other times it was a thirty-minute, long-distance phone call that he would ask if he could make to his big sister at college, a call certainly worth the cost.

Since his communication style was different from his sister's, it took longer for him to let us know what was happening. As parents we could see that there was something on his mind. But it took him a while to get it out. I'd sometimes ask him to go along for the ride when I'd have to drive somewhere on an errand. Or I'd go to his room at night and stretch out on his bed, just to let him know I was interested in what was going on and had plenty of time to listen. Many a discussion started with: "How was your night last night?"

A Listening Ear

The first step is to be available, but that availability will be wasted if the parent does most of the talking. This is no time to lecture. This is a time to fill in the gaps in your teen's understanding of the dating process and of the opposite sex. As the teen begins to recap an evening's events, and there seem to be areas where a parent might have concerns, save the questions for another time. This is feedback time, a time for the child to talk and the parent to listen. Get the whole picture. Don't frustrate your child with questions and comments to the point where they just quit and go to bed. Keeping these lines of communication open requires restraint and patience. The teen needs to feel confident that the parent wants to hear about the night and won't critique it.

While listening, hold your heart. "I sit there listening," a mother recalled wistfully, "and I am once again reminded of just how much my son is growing up. I want to hear everything, but then again I don't. The first time my son told me that he had kissed his date good-night, my heart just fell out my back. I was glad he felt free and open enough to tell me this, so I worked hard at keeping a calm, approving look on my face. It wasn't easy, but I want him to always feel comfortable talking to me, so I have to be open to what he tells me."

But what happens when they tell us something awful, something we don't agree with? Do we just sit and listen and smile and nod our heads? No, we are entitled—no, responsible—to let our teen know that we disagree with an activity or a stand they have taken. But we need to disagree in a way that will keep the doors of communication open.

Yelling across the family room, "You were where?!" or "They were drinking what?!" isn't the way to do it. Instead, listen without interrupting, wait for the proper time, then ask some questions about the party, about your child's reaction to the problem.

"You said that there was a lot of beer at the party at Jack's house. How did you feel about that?" It's important to first see if they have been thinking through that circumstance.

Then continue with a question such as, "How do you think your mom and I, or your date's parents, feel about that?"

Use silence to encourage your child to answer. Fight the urge to go ahead and answer the questions yourself or fill the gap with more questions. Look at your child and just wait. Be pleasant. Open. Another question you might get to is: "What do you think you will do differently the next time you arrive at a party where that is happening?" Remember, this is time for training, not punishment. This is not the time to begin restricting a teen's parameters on dating. Parents can find out a great deal about how their children are doing by being available and by keeping a listening ear. Your follow-up questions should prompt your children to do some of their own evaluation of a date.

Listen for the Unspoken

Post-date feedback time is a perfect opportunity to answer a child's unspoken questions about the opposite sex, differences that may puzzle them. Everyone begins thinking they know about the opposite sex. Aren't they just like we are? But then something catches them off guard. They don't understand why something happened.

Annie came in from her date and her mom had a pot of herbal tea ready and waiting. The tea had become a tradition for their post-date talks. When Annie walked into the room, her mother could tell that her daughter had had a great time on the date by the way Annie bounced into the room. But there was something else she noticed. She knew her daughter well enough to know that all she had to do was wait and listen.

Annie spent twenty minutes telling her mom about the party, the great time she had had with her date, who had been at the party, what they did. Then Annie was quiet, just sipping her tea, looking at the tea, not at her mother. "He kissed me good-night," she said. It had been their fourth date, and Annie's mother didn't see anything wrong with that. But obviously something was bothering Annie.

"It seems like something else happened," Annie's mother said. "You're awfully quiet."

Annie didn't say anything for a long time. Neither did her mother. "Well, it was kind of strange," Annie said finally. "He didn't just kiss me good-night. He French-kissed me." She wrinkled up her nose a little and looked over at her mother. "That really caught me off guard. I don't know what to think. I didn't really like it."

That night Annie and her mother stayed up for hours, talking about the things they had talked about many times before: the difference in dating from the boy's point of view and from the girl's. Annie had heard most of it before. In fact, her mother started their discussion with, "I know you already know this, but let me see if I can help you understand some things about boys." But that night, the information was of significantly more interest than before, now that Annie was dating and right in the middle of the differences between the genders. What her mother was telling her now was relevant. Annie asked more questions. The answers now made more sense. She learned about the signals that she might be giving off to her date without even realizing that she was doing it. She also learned to watch for some signals that boys give out. Annie's mother took advantage of their post-date talk time to teach her child about getting along with other people.

As the post-date discussions continue, you'll begin to notice that your relationship with your child begins to shift. It's a time when the young person is breaking free of the parent, testing their wings on the outside. They want to be free, but they also want that connection with parents, a safe haven to return to when the outside world gets a little scary. By listening to their stories, you're offering your child encouragement and permission to reach for more freedom.

This is not a time to be naïve. This is a time to be wise. Be patient. Listen. Learn about how your child is progressing in accepting the responsibilities of dating. Under some circumstances, you might have to step right back into a strong parenting role and be restrictive. Be careful. Listen to the whole story first. If you don't you're likely to close the door to communication, or you could teach your child a very manipulative form of communication.

"It was just a game we would play," a twenty-six-year-old woman said during a counseling session. "My dad would stay up to talk to me. I knew if I told him what I did, he'd be very judgmental. Even if I wasn't doing anything wrong but I was at the same party where someone might be doing something wrong, he'd give me a lecture about not being at those parties. So I just told him what I knew he wanted to hear. That way everyone was happy. The problem was that I started going down hill and had no one to talk to or to keep me from falling. We just kept playing the game."

Don't play the game. Keep an open ear and know when it's time to jump in. There's a great payoff for both parent and child. Parents will have a better idea of what's really going on in their child's life. And the child will be able to ask questions and get answers when they need them, while they are in the midst of the dating process.

The By-Product

It was 11:30, a Saturday night, when the phone rang. Late-night phone calls tend to bring bad news, so they always scare me a little. I jumped up, answered the phone, and heard my daughter's voice. She was then a freshman in a college, 1,012 miles away from home.

"Hi, Dad!" she said as if it were eight in the evening.

"Hi, Honey. Is everything okay?" I asked quickly, holding my breath, amazed at how long it seemed to take for her to answer.

"Oh, for sure, Dad!" she said, bubbling over with excitement while I was trying to breathe and sound normal. "I just got in from my first college date. Can I talk to Mom?"

Summary

1. When your children are dating, be available when they get home to listen to how their evening went—what they did, who was there—and to answer any questions they might have. It's a golden opportunity. Don't miss it.

2. Your child will somehow select one parent to talk to after a date. And it's not the parent who talks the most, it's the parent who has proven to be the best listener.

3. Not every child wants to talk when they return home from a date. If yours doesn't, then look for a time when you can have a post-date discussion, maybe during a quiet time the next day. Just don't miss the opportunity for discussion.

4. Don't lecture. Instead, listen to what your child is saying. Try to understand what your child is not saying.

5. Be prepared to answer the questions your child may have about the differences between boys and girls.

Questions to Ask Yourself

1. Which parent does my teen tend to gravitate to when facing a difficult decision?

2. When is the best time for me to have a post-date discussion with my child? Is my child a morning person or a late-night person?
3. Is there anything I do as a parent that makes it difficult for my teen to feel comfortable talking about certain things with me? Am I too quick to judge or give lectures? Am I embarrassed?
4. Is there a story or a humorous anecdote about my dating life that I could tell my teen? (Sometimes a story makes the point you're trying to get across. If your child is upset about breaking up with someone, the right story about one of your breakups might let them know that you can understand their pain, but that they will, eventually, feel better.

Part 4

The Lessons Learned

Chapter 17

Now You May Because Now You Can

"Dad?" Torrey said as she walked into my study. "Jack wants to know if I can go out to dinner with him and then to a movie. He just called."

"Sure," I said. "Just make sure you let us know when you'll be home."

Torrey started to leave, then she stopped and turned around. "Can I ask you a question, Dad?"

"Sure."

"Why did you say yes without even asking where we were going or what movie we were going to go see?"

"What do you mean?" I said.

"Not too long ago, I would ask you if I could go somewhere and you would give me the third degree."

"The third degree?" I said, giving her a look that asked if I really had been that bad.

"Well, maybe not the third degree, but you sure used to want to know everything about where I was going before you'd give your okay. Now all I do is ask and you say it's okay. Didn't you trust me before?"

"It's not that I all of a sudden trust you now and didn't trust you before," I explained. "It's that I feel confident that you know how to date. Before when you would ask our permission to go out on a date, you were saying 'May I?' The real question we wanted to find the answer to was 'Can I?' Are you able to date? And you've proven that you are. So I don't need all the details anymore. It's easy for me to say, 'Yes, you may,' because we both know that now you *can*."

This book has been based on the premise that a parent needs to be sure their child "can date." The child needs the ability and understanding of how to date properly. The child needs practice dating. All this is accomplished through a training program that parents set up and supervise. The training teaches our children about dating relationships and about personal control and responsibilities. Having learned these very important lessons, our teens are then able to date in a manner that is pleasing to God.

Establishing the process of teaching a child about dating is a job with a definite deadline. Parents need to start and finish the job while the child is still living at home. The best time to work through a proper progression of dating, from group activities and double dates to the "real" date, with just two, is when the children are in high school. Every child needs to learn just what their personal responsibilities are when dating.

This parent-directed "dating course" works. Without it, or something like it, our teens will be responding to only their passions and their peers. You wouldn't just flip the car keys to your child when they ask to learn how to drive. You shouldn't turn them loose in dating without first making sure that you've taught them what they need to know. "Yes, you may" has little to do with the more important answer: "Yes, you can."

Start early. Start now. Start wherever you and your children are in the dating process. Don't wait. Be involved now. Your children need to know how to live their lives—and how to date—in a manner that is pleasing to Christ.

Learning to date in a proper manner has a lifelong effect. Look around you. How many couples have we all met who married for the wrong reasons? Or because they had to? How many of these couples began dating without any preparation, any guidance? How many immediately began dating the wrong person for them? These mistakes in dating, which usually started when they were teenagers, follow them for the rest of their lives.

A Final Story

Peter arrived at a college in the Midwest with his commitment to purity intact. He knew that God had a special plan for his life. He was certain of it. Peter had even made his own personal marriage list that included just what kind of a woman he would want to marry. While in high school his parents had taught him about dating, but he had only been out a few times. He didn't have much experience. But now, in college, he was ready to date. In fact, Peter was ready for everything but the handling of his own heart.

Shortly after arriving at college, Peter met Barbara and they started dating. Barbara was beautiful and fun to be with, but she was also much more worldly in her approach to dating. Over a period of about a year, Peter and Barbara became very close. Peter was able to stay pure during that year only because of his commitment to God. He knew that he had fallen in love with a girl who met none of the top qualifications on his marriage list, but somehow that didn't seem to matter. Church was not something Barbara was interested in.

As things became serious, Peter was encouraged by his parents to come home for a long weekend. He knew they were going to pounce on him about the many differences that existed between him and Barbara. But they surprised him. They didn't attack.

The first night Peter was home, they all went out to dinner and the topic of discussion, naturally, was his relationship with Barbara. He did tell them that he thought he was in love with her. When they didn't react the way he thought they would, he went on to admit that there were some differences in the way he and Barbara viewed things.

"Like what?" his dad asked. "Perhaps these are differences that aren't that important." His dad knew full well that there were dramatic philosophical differences, but he wanted two things: He wanted his son to be able to talk about those differences, and he wanted to avoid a possible argument, with his son trying to defend those differences. "How does Barbara match up with the top things on your list?"

Peter went down the first three things on the list, the three things he had believed were most important. No matter how hard he tried to make Barbara fit the list, he had to admit, at least to himself, that she didn't match up with any of the things that he had said were most important.

"It seems to me that you have a difficult decision to make, son," Peter's dad said very gently. "Either you have changed and this list doesn't matter anymore, or you have ignored your list. Either way, you need to make a decision quickly before it's too late. We will be praying with you this weekend and ask God to help you see his plan for your life."

The rest of the weekend was great. Peter had a wonderful time with his parents. In fact, he remembered thinking that this was just like old times, though he couldn't push out of his mind the difficult decision he had to make.

He went back to the campus, having told his parents that he just didn't know what to do. Peter did think that he loved Barbara. His parents continued to pray for him and call him every few days. Though it was a time of agony for them, they knew that Peter was an adult and had to make this most difficult decision on his own.

Finally Peter realized that he had to end the relationship with Barbara. His past training and the discussions with his parents helped him to realize that either everything he believed was true and his heart was betraying him, or his heart was right and he would have to walk away from what he believed. He knew Barbara and his list couldn't coexist. If he married Barbara, he would be settling for less than what God had planned for him.

The year after breaking up with Barbara was the worst year of Peter's life. In fact, he even changed colleges. Peter graduated from the second college and went off to seminary, never really dating anyone seriously. From time to time he still thought about Barbara, wondering if he had made a mistake. By sticking with what he believed, was he now destined to remain single the rest of his life? Was his list too rigid?

Peter finally did find a young woman who fit the criteria of his list. Her name is Diane. They met during his last year of seminary and eventually were married. Together they now serve in a church in Michigan.

Looking back on it, Peter is grateful that his parents taught him about dating, about figuring out what kind of woman he should marry. He now knows that he almost made a terrible mistake back in college. He almost let his feelings overrule what his head was telling him, that Barbara was not the right one for him.

Peter kept his commitment to purity, giving it as a most precious gift to his wife, Diane. Peter's training and his commitment proved to be stronger than his feelings. They kept him on track when he so easily could have taken another path in life.

Today he's grateful for that training, for believing early on that God had a purpose for his life—a mission.

You May

"May" is a permission word. "May" gives a person permission to do something. It too often takes for granted that the person "can" do something. Is able to do something.

But there's one more factor that we must recognize. After a person has been taught how to do something, they "can." When they have permission to do it, they "may." But neither factor guarantees that they "will do" whatever it is in a safe and proper manner.

In dating, a person may have been taught everything about dating. They have permission to date. They know what to do and how to do it. The final question depends on the individual. Ultimately, we each decide our own course in life. We do not have to do what we've been taught. When we're alone, we can still drive recklessly. We can still handle a date any way we want. We can still fail to do the right thing.

"So why bother?" one parent said in exasperation. "Why bother going through all these years of training—and hassle, I might add—only to have them go out there and fail?"

What that father was really saying was, "If I can't control the outcome, I don't want to be a part of the process."

A proverb says, "Train a child in the way he should go, and when he is old he will not turn from it" (Proverbs 22:6). That's a very wise saying for parents to heed. It's not a promise. There are many promises in the Bible, but the Proverbs are not promises, they are instead wise sayings for people to live by.

As a child, if no one ever teaches me, I won't have any lessons to draw on when I need them. But if someone does take the time to teach me, then I have the opportunity to draw on that training. If my parents not only teach me the things I need to know but also teach me the concept of responsibility, then I am prepared. I'm prepared with knowledge as well as the discipline to follow through with the things I know I ought to do. I then have an opportunity to succeed at being the kind of person I was meant to be.

"And what is that?" What is it that our young people need to be when they grow up? Beginning in Genesis 37 there is that story of the young Jewish boy named Joseph. He didn't know what he was supposed to be when he grew up, but he did know how he was supposed to be *while* he was growing up. He knew he was to handle his life in a way that would be pleasing to God. He knew he needed to work hard. He knew he needed to remain pure. He also knew that the rest was up to God. Nothing could have prepared him for the things that would happen to him when he was seventeen. He could never have guessed that his brothers would be so jealous of him that they would sell him into slavery. He didn't know that he would be ripped out of his affluent home and transplanted as a slave in Egypt. Nor could he have guessed that for years, as a slave, he would be working for a man whose wife would try, day after day, to seduce Joseph.

Joseph wasn't prepared for the specific circumstances that he faced in life. But he was prepared with proper answers to whatever circumstances came at him. His focal point in life was not his loneliness. His attitude was not, "Does anybody know what I'm dealing with here?" His desire was not to comfort his loneliness by giving in to the constant advances of his boss's wife. Joseph's focal point in life was to be pleasing to God in all that he did. That became his quest.

He decided that the rest was up to God. He would work hard at the tasks that were put before him. He left his future up to God. Joseph took on the responsibility for the specific tasks he saw before him. He was responsible for his own purity.

With that focus, God was able to use Joseph in a mighty way, even to the point of taking him from being a prisoner to becoming the second most powerful man in Egypt, second only to the pharaoh. All in one day.

God has a plan for each person. His plan is bigger than dating. But the proper teaching of the dating process is extremely important because it has impact on the rest of a young person's life. Improper dating, and thus a lack of purity, can easily derail that plan.

Ed sat in my office staring out the window as he talked. "I knew two things when I started college. I knew that God had called me to be a pastor. I also knew that it would be very important to find the right girl to join me in that kind of work. What did I know about girls and dating? Nothing. My parents had been missionaries in the jungles of Brazil. I had never had a date in my life until I came to the States to go to college. Emma was the first girl I ever went out with. I was so unprepared to handle my feelings for her.

"Soon after we started dating I knew she was definitely not the girl to be a pastor's wife. But she was beautiful and we quickly became sexually involved. I married Emma for all the wrong reasons. I married Emma because of my eyes and my biology. Our eleven years of marriage have been a nightmare for both of us. I think the fact that I went on anyway and became a pastor, against her wishes, is one of the reasons why she has had multiple affairs these past years. She's rebelling against me and everything I stand for."

Ed sat for a moment, his head down, not saying a word. Then he looked up. "I had no idea what dating was all about. I didn't really have any idea where our dating would lead. Now my poor choices have destroyed everything." With that Ed buried his face in his hands and wept.

Dating is a very difficult "playing field" to step out onto. No caring, responsible parent would ever want to send their children out onto that field without first making sure that they were properly equipped and prepared. No parent should ever send their young person out onto that field without making sure that their child knows who the Coach is and that the teen should be dating for him. Knowing the answers to these questions will impact the rest of a child's life.

One day when Torrey wanted to go shopping she asked, "Can I drive the car?" The proper answer to her question was, "Yes, you may, because now you can. Just make sure that you do what you are now trained and responsible to do."

I was able to say that to her, to transfer the responsibility to her, because of the training program we had for learning to drive. We went through a long process of training with her so that we would eventually be able to say, with confidence, "Yes, now you can."

I want to feel as confident about the training we give them on dating. I want to feel confident that they learn not only how to date but also the responsibilities of dating. When our daughter and son move onto a college campus, into an adult world of dating, I want to wave good-bye, knowing that I've done my job as a parent, I've taught them what they need to know about dating. I want to be able to say, "I'm glad I did!" rather than "I wish I had!"

FOR MORE INFORMATION

Dr. Bob Barnes and his wife, Rosemary Barnes, have written other books that will help your family. These books can be purchased or ordered from a bookstore near you.

Great Sexpectations (with Rosemary Barnes)
Raising Confident Kids
Ready for Responsibility
Rock-Solid Marriage (with Rosemary Barnes)
We Need to Talk (with Rosemary Barnes)
Who's in Charge Here?
Winning the Heart of Your Stepchild

The Barnses also conduct parenting or marriage seminars all across North America. For more information on the seminars, books, or tapes, please call 1-800-838-1552 or write:

Dr. Robert Barnes
Sheridan House Family Ministries
4200 S. W. 54 Ct.
Ft. Lauderdale, FL 33314

Who's in Charge Here?
Overcoming Power Struggles with Your Kids

DR. BOB BARNES

Have you found yourself giving in too often, yelling too much, or making excuses for your child's behavior? Here's how to establish order and harmony in your home and avoid power struggles.

The key, says author Bob Barnes, is to have a family plan of shared responsibilities and consequences so that your children know what is expected of them. Read, and learn, how to create a plan and how to respond when your child fails to meet the plan—when he or she lies, argues with siblings, fails at a task, or faces peer pressure. Barnes shows you how to discipline your children with consistency and love without feeling guilty or causing anger or resentment.

Who's in Charge Here? will help you establish a pattern of positive behavior and self-control that will get your home back in order and avoid disaster. By arming yourself with this book you can win each "battle" without losing the "war."

Softcover: 0-310-21743-1

ZondervanPublishingHouse
Grand Rapids, Michigan 49530
http://www.zondervan.com

Winning the Heart of Your Stepchild

DR. BOB BARNES

"I've got the love to give.
Now how can I get my stepchild to accept it?"

Does that question sound familiar? Whether you are presently a stepparent, a dating single parent, or in the courtship stage before marriage, the challenge of blending families is one of the most difficult you will ever face.

Winning the Heart of Your Stepchild is a hands-on guidebook for today's men and women who face the special challenge of blending families. Because children must process so many emotions and thoughts—guilt over the divorce, unrealistic expectations, a sense of panic or fear—parents must learn to interpret those feelings and behaviors for any new family to succeed.

This book shows how to:

— create an open atmosphere in the home
— give reassuring answers to a child's questions
— become a strong team with your new spouse
— deal with the inevitable challenges to a new authority figure
— build a foundation of love, understanding, and personal discipline that will make your new family special

Winning the Heart of Your Stepchild provides an indispensable road map for new moms and dads who want one vibrant, happy, blended family.

Softcover: 0-310-21804-7

ZondervanPublishingHouse
Grand Rapids, Michigan 49530
http://www.zondervan.com

We want to hear from you. Please send your comments about
this book to us in care of the address below. Thank you.

ZondervanPublishingHouse
Grand Rapids, Michigan 49530
http://www.zondervan.com